Published in 2018 by

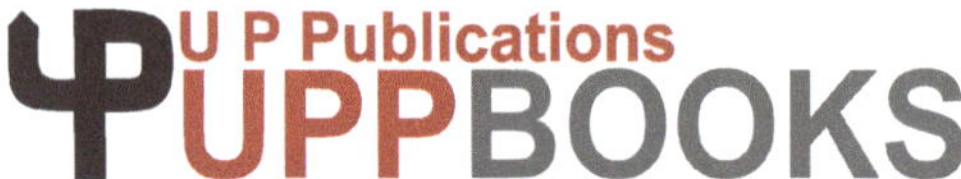

U P Publications, St George's House,
George Street, Huntingdon,
Cambridgeshire, PE29 3GH
+44 208 133 0123
manager@uppublications.ltd.uk
www.uppbooks.com

A catalogue record for this book is available from the British Library
Replaces ISBN 978-1-388933-52-4
This is a New Edition

Hardback ISBN 13: 978-1-912777-04-4
eBook ISBN 13: 978-1-912777-05-1

Printed in England by The Lightning Source Group
www.balkancaffeination.com
www.uppbooks.com

BALKAN CAFFEINATION

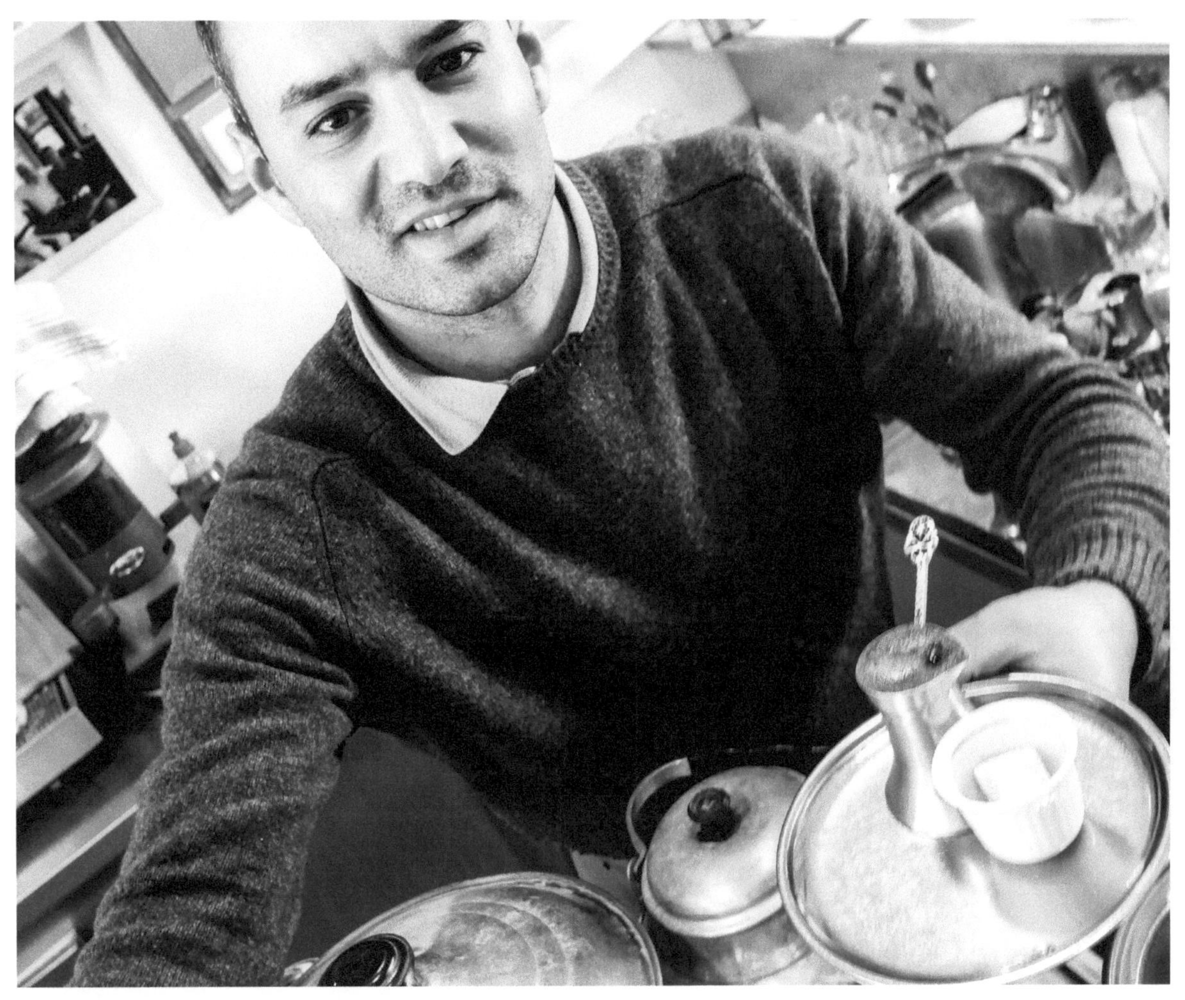

a caffeinated photo-journal by

Paul Kelly and Fred Shively

BALKAN CAFFEINATION

Foreword

Few places on earth put greater importance on coffee, in everyday life, than the Balkans. Here, coffee is not just a pleasurable interlude or a break from work; it animates the very heart of Balkan culture. More a ritual than a drink, it's invariably coffee first, business later. Coffee is conversation and connection; coffee 'to go' is almost a social crime (with the possible exception of Bulgaria).

Coffee has been here a long time: it first came ashore, on its maiden voyage into Europe from Yemen, around the 16th century. On the way, its preparation and serving style had already been transformed as it travelled through Egypt and Istanbul.

As coffee/café lovers and inveterate travellers, we wanted to follow the caffeine trail through this historically turbulent, wildly beautiful, warm-hearted and sometimes mysterious region.

What follows is a photographic journey of discovery. Our first visit took in Bosnia-Herzegovina, Serbia, Bulgaria and Romania. Perhaps in future we can complete the picture with visits to Albania, Croatia, Greece, Kosovo, Macedonia, Montenegro and Slovenia.

So pour yourself a cup of your favourite brew and join us. We hope that our images and encounters capture the everyday celebration of coffee and its unique place in Balkan culture.

Paul Kelly and Fred Shively

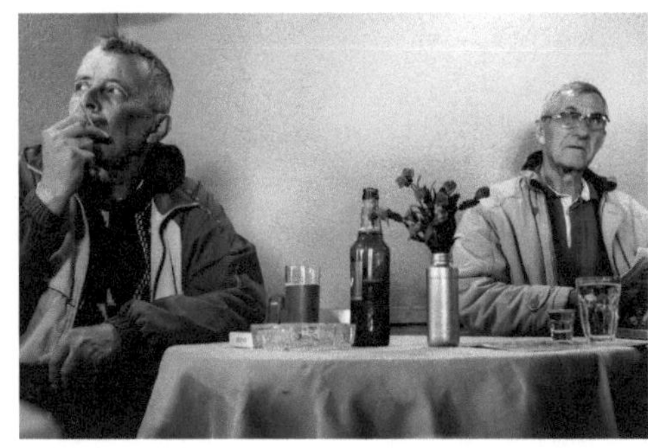
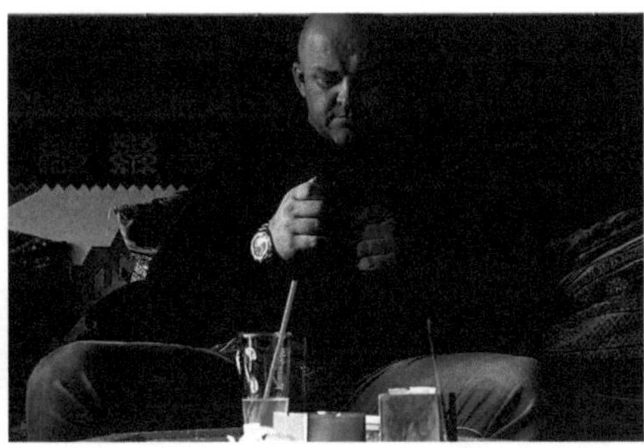
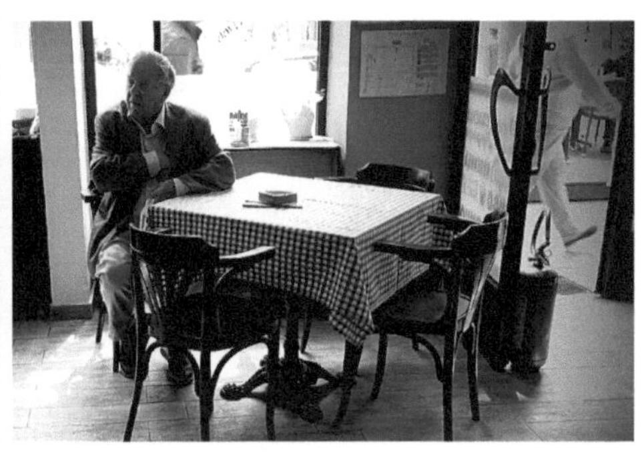
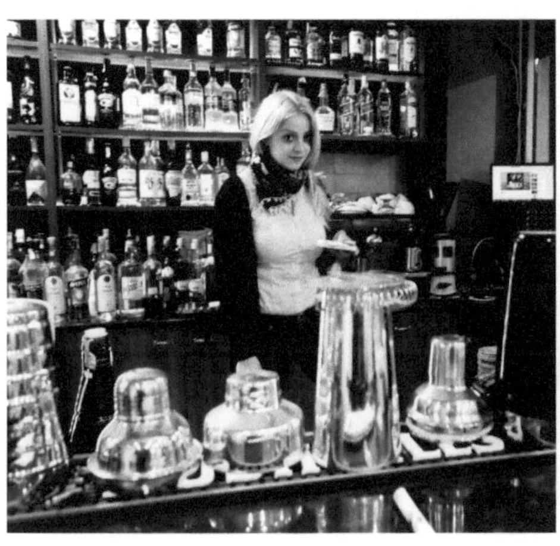
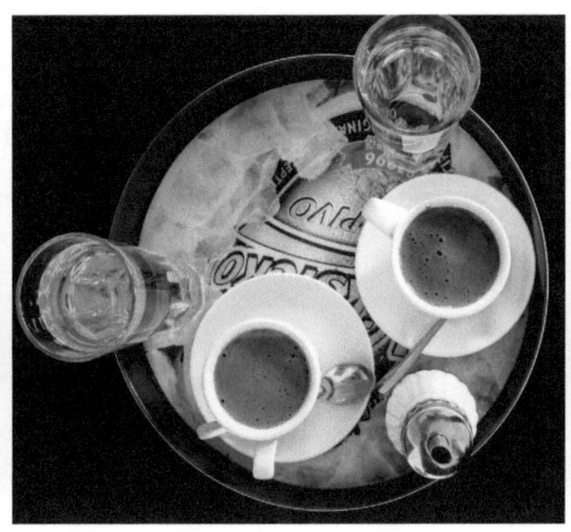
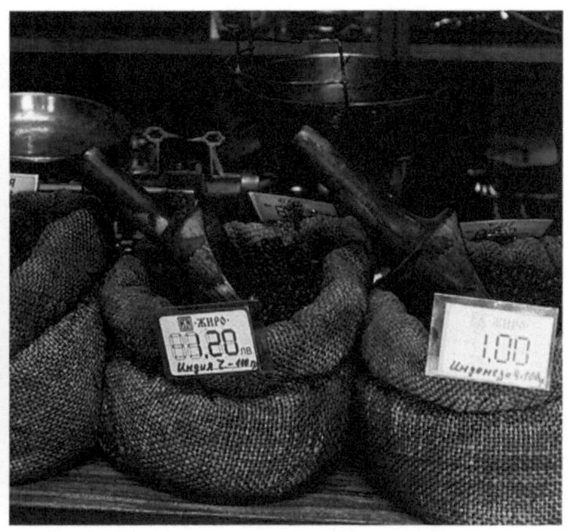
·ЖИРО·
1,20 лв
1.00
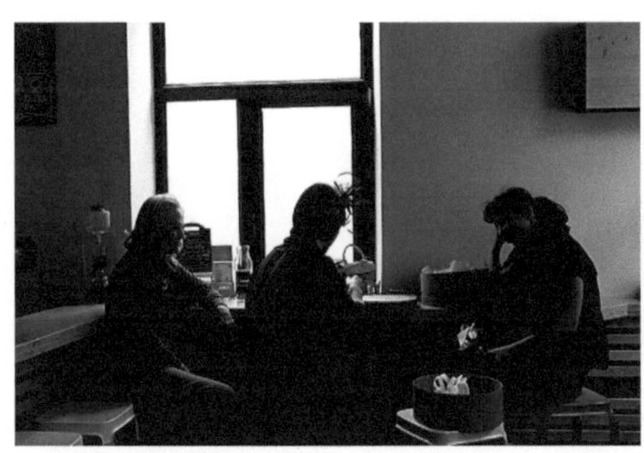
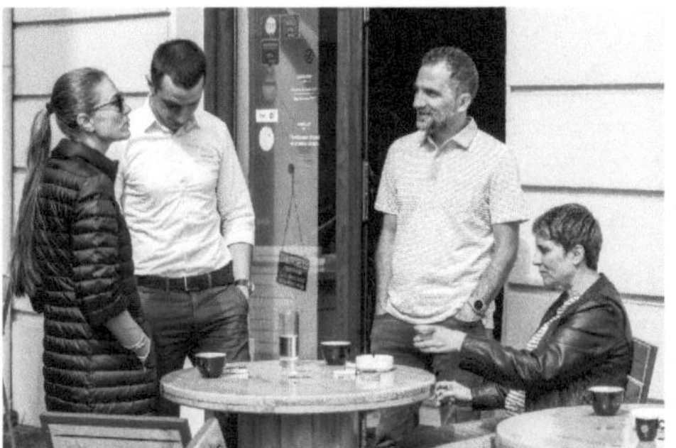
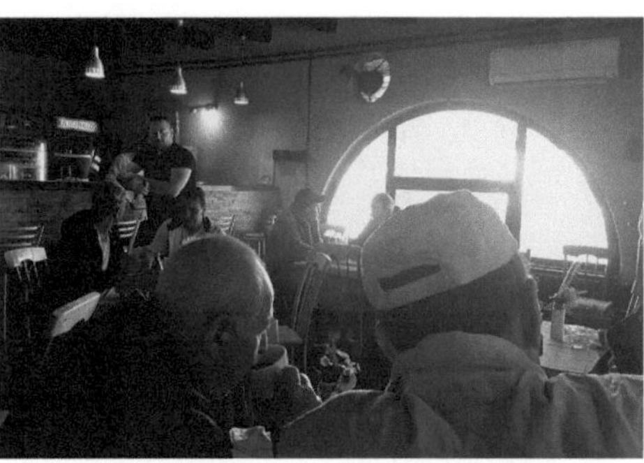

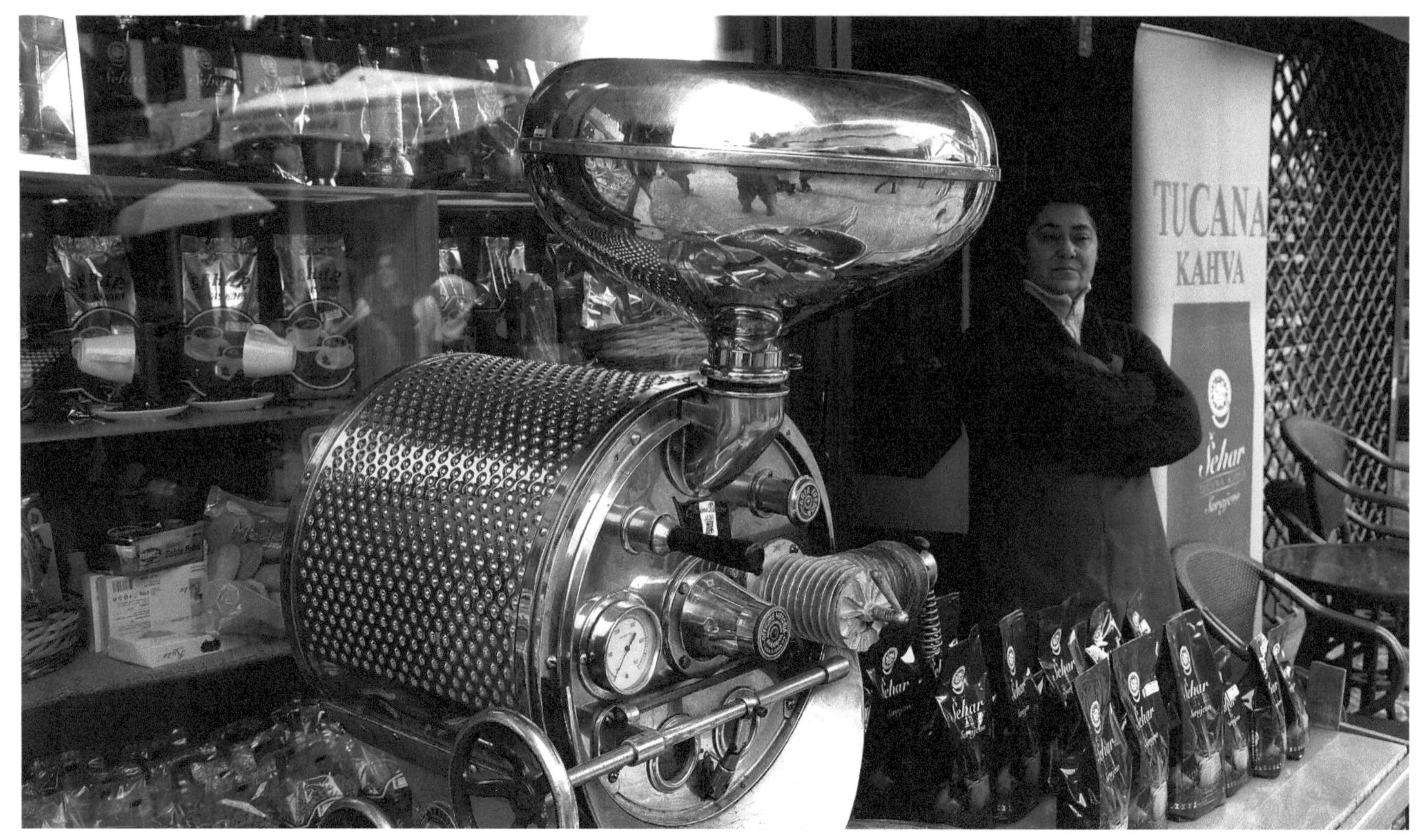

photograph by Fred Shively

SARAJEVO, BOSNIA AND HERZEGOVINA - Coffee roaster/grinder/purveyor Tucana. One of many kahva outlets in the bascarsija (old town) quarter of Sarajevo, Bosnia and Herzegovina. The grinds are generally ultra fine for use in the traditional Bosnian method of brewing.

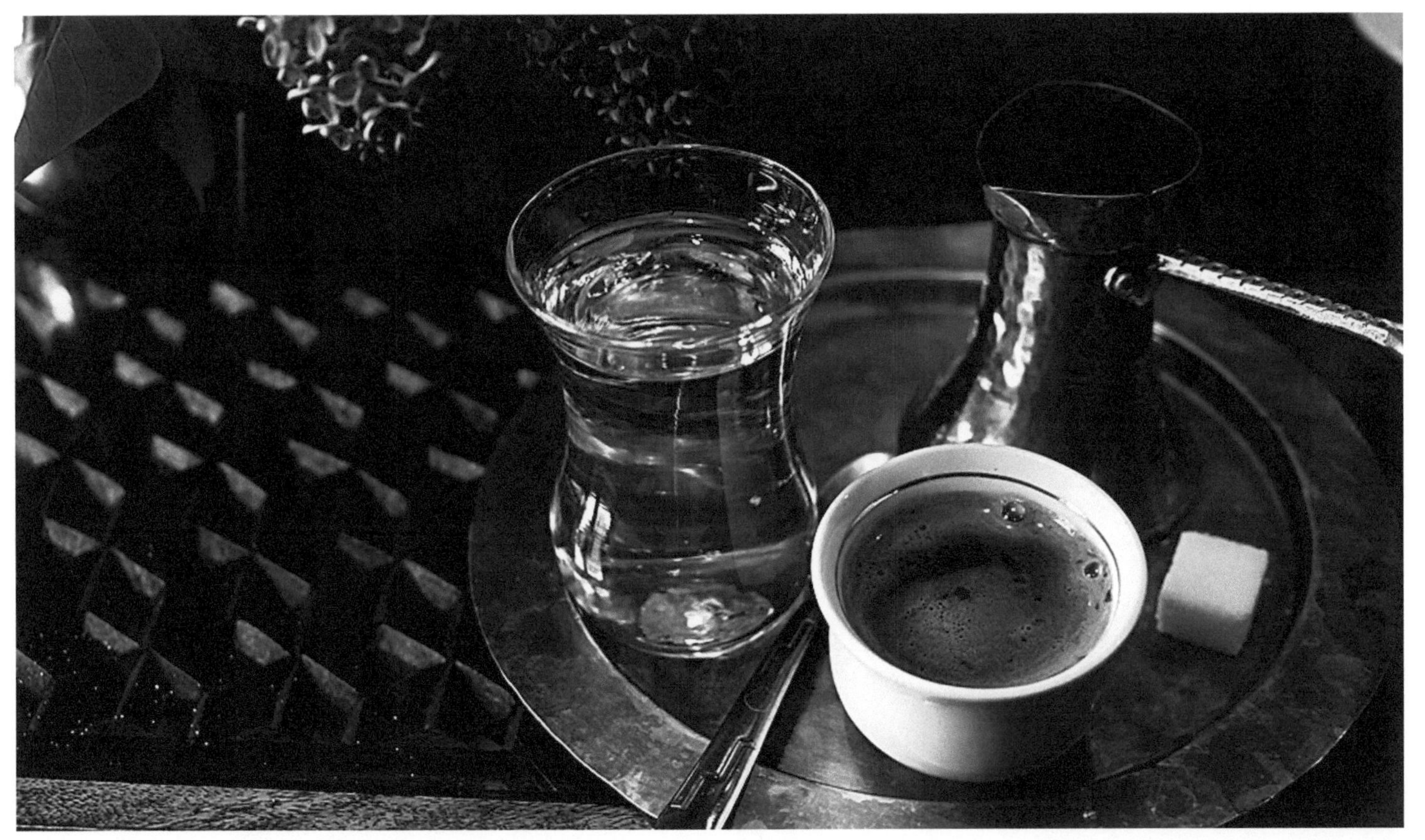

photograph by Fred Shively

SARAJEVO - Café Djulistan. As per its Ottoman legacy, traditional coffee in Bosnia and Herzegovina is a potent brew made in a copper or brass, tin-lined djezve. Pour, sip, nibble the sugar cube. The accompanying glass of water is almost obligatory, particularly for the uninitiated.

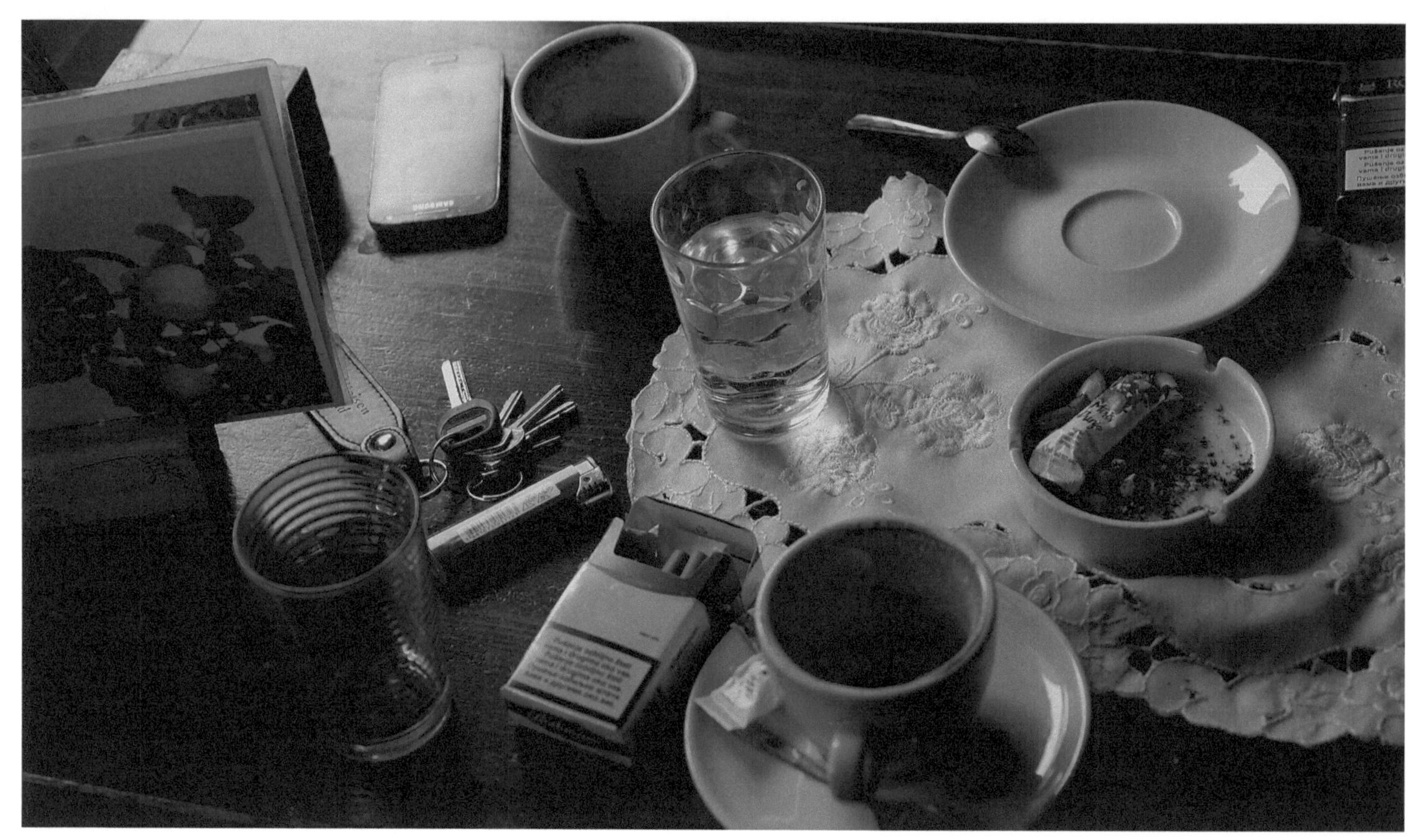

photograph by Fred Shively

SARAJEVO - Café Miras Dunja. Remains of a typical morning coffee break. Sipping and smoking still go hand in hand in many, if not most, Balkan cafés.

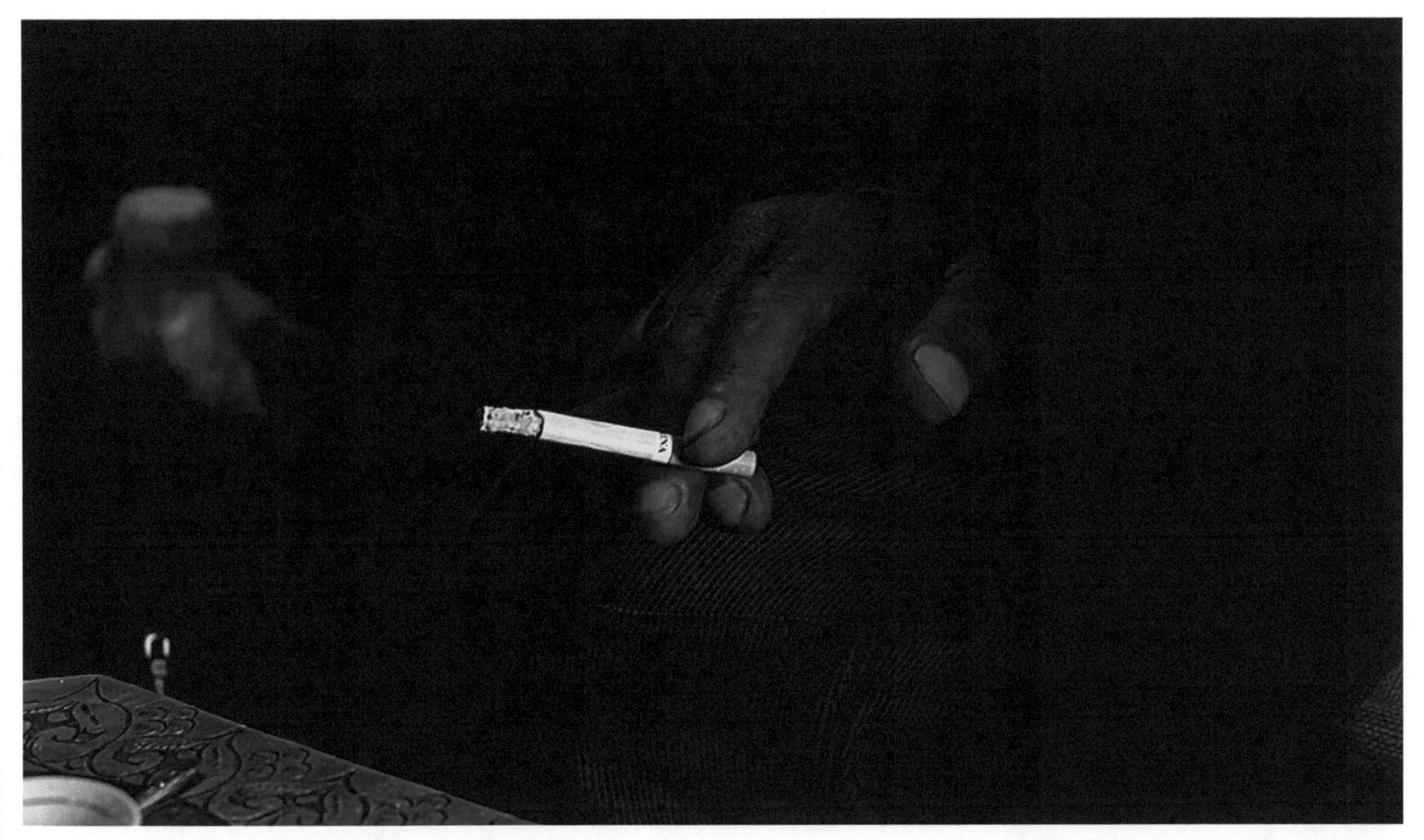

photograph by Fred Shively

SARAJEVO - Essential accessory to coffee drinking at Café Index, favourite haunt of the coppersmiths in the Bascarsija quarter of Sarajevo. Barely a non-smoker among the regular patrons!

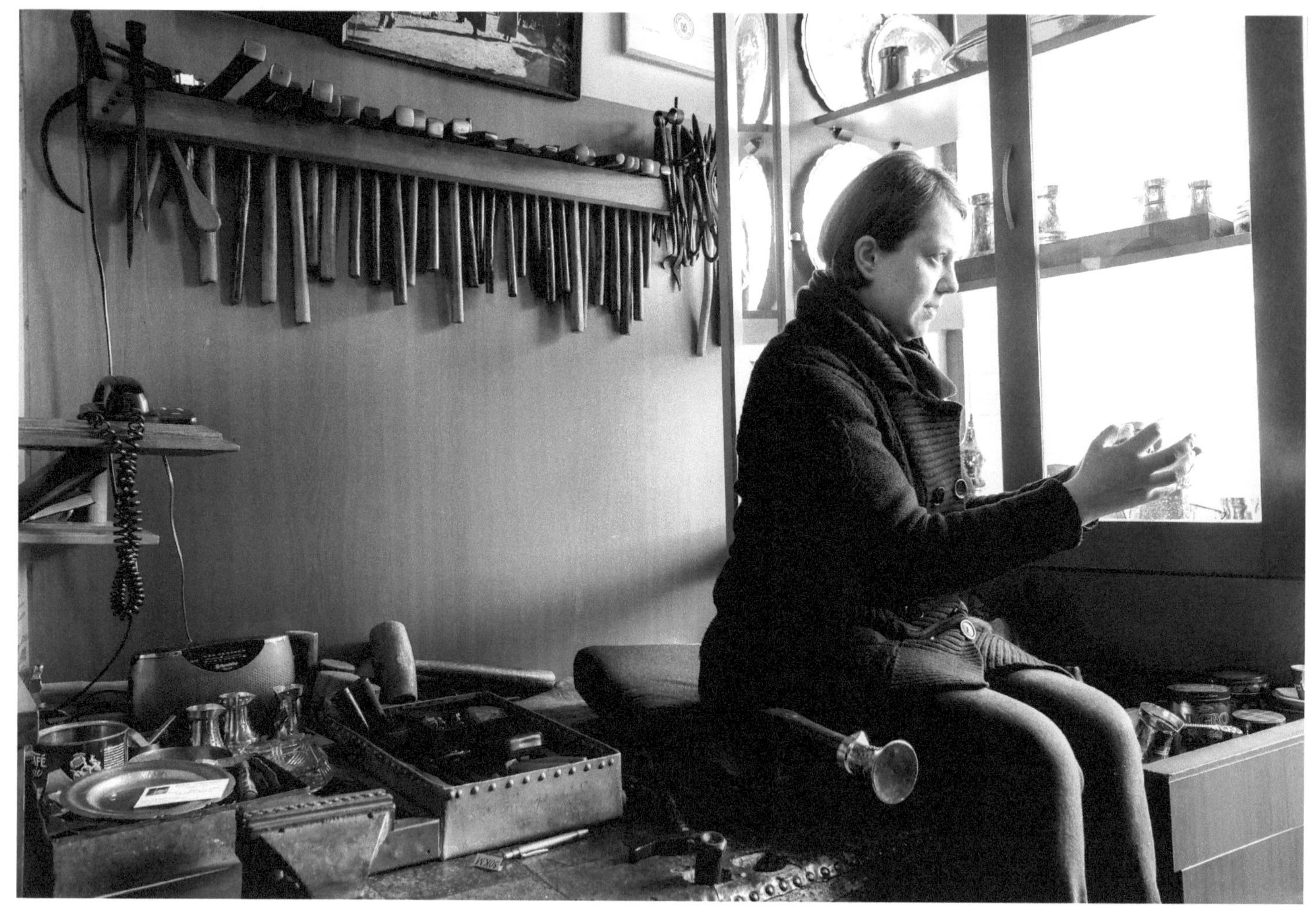

photograph by Paul Kelly

SARAJEVO - In the Bascarsija the centuries old craft of making djezves normally falls to men. Nermina Alic is the only woman coppersmith in town. Nermina works from her tiny workshop in 'Blacksmith' street. She owns the only remaining wood-fired smelter, to render the tin for lining her products.

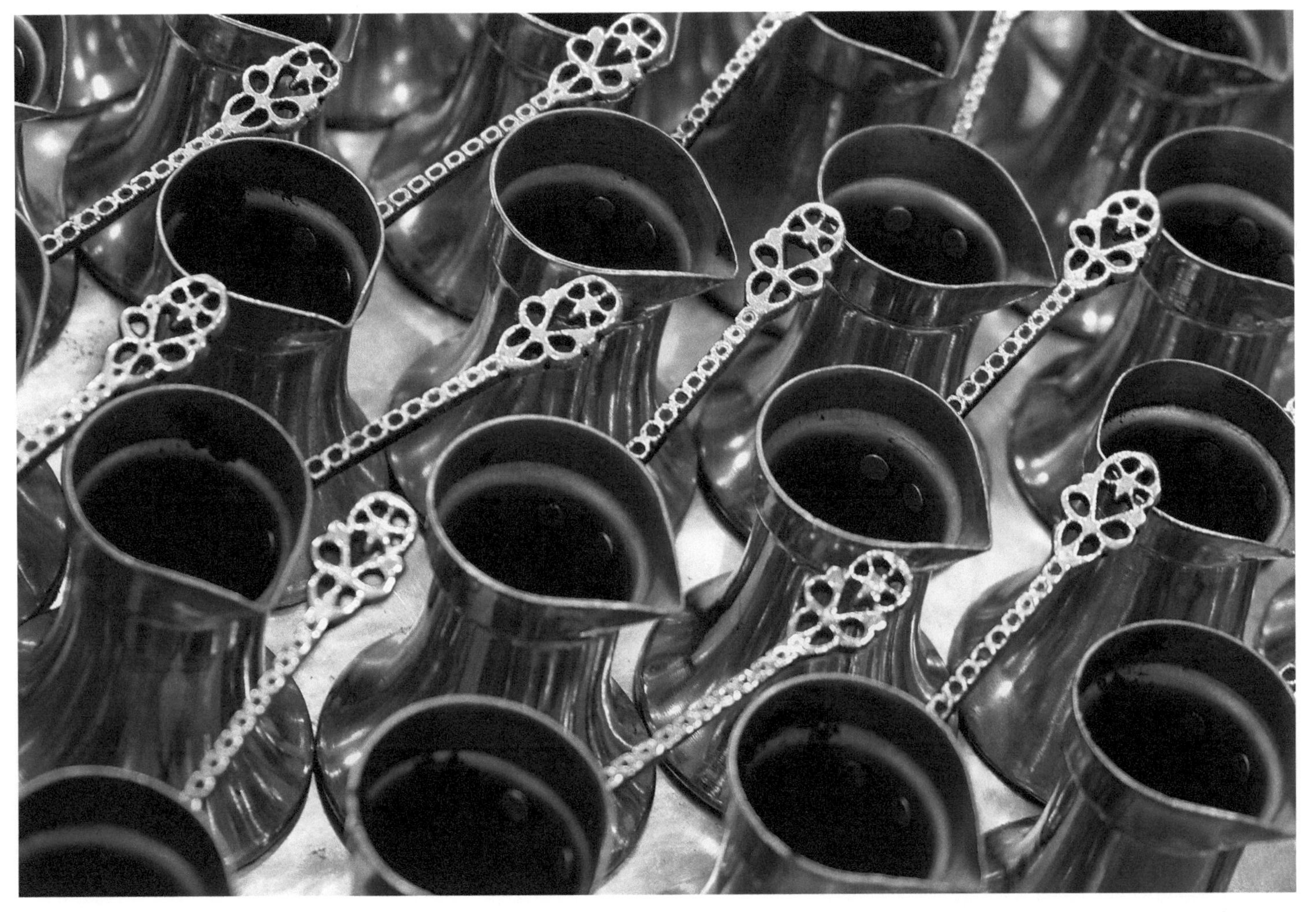

photograph by Fred Shively

SARAJEVO - Café Tunel. Ranks of djezves ready for the morning rush.

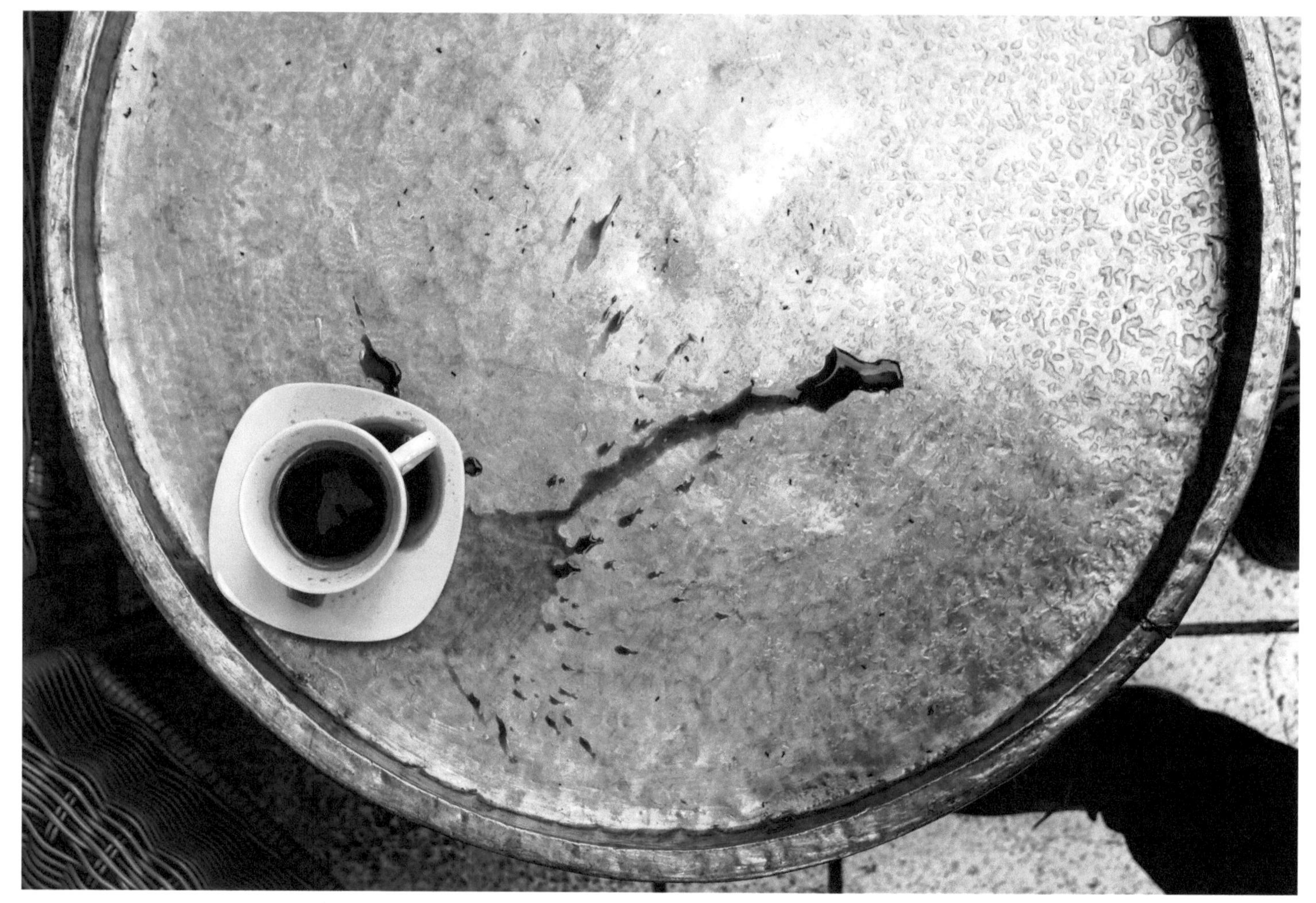

photograph by Paul Kelly

SARAJEVO - Café Djulistan. A bit of Bosnian lore: if you spill coffee on a table and the spill comes to you, you will marry an attractive partner. No existing marriages were harmed in this particular spill!

SARAJEVO - Gallery Boris Smoje is part café, part art gallery.

Owner Goran Esapović's (right) father was a famous Bosnian actor who, years ago, wanted a gallery for local artists. The art gallery alone didn't make much money so Goran evolved Gallery Boris Smoje into the unpretentious and laidback café it is today.

"You can't live in this city without coffee. it is the way of life", says Goran.

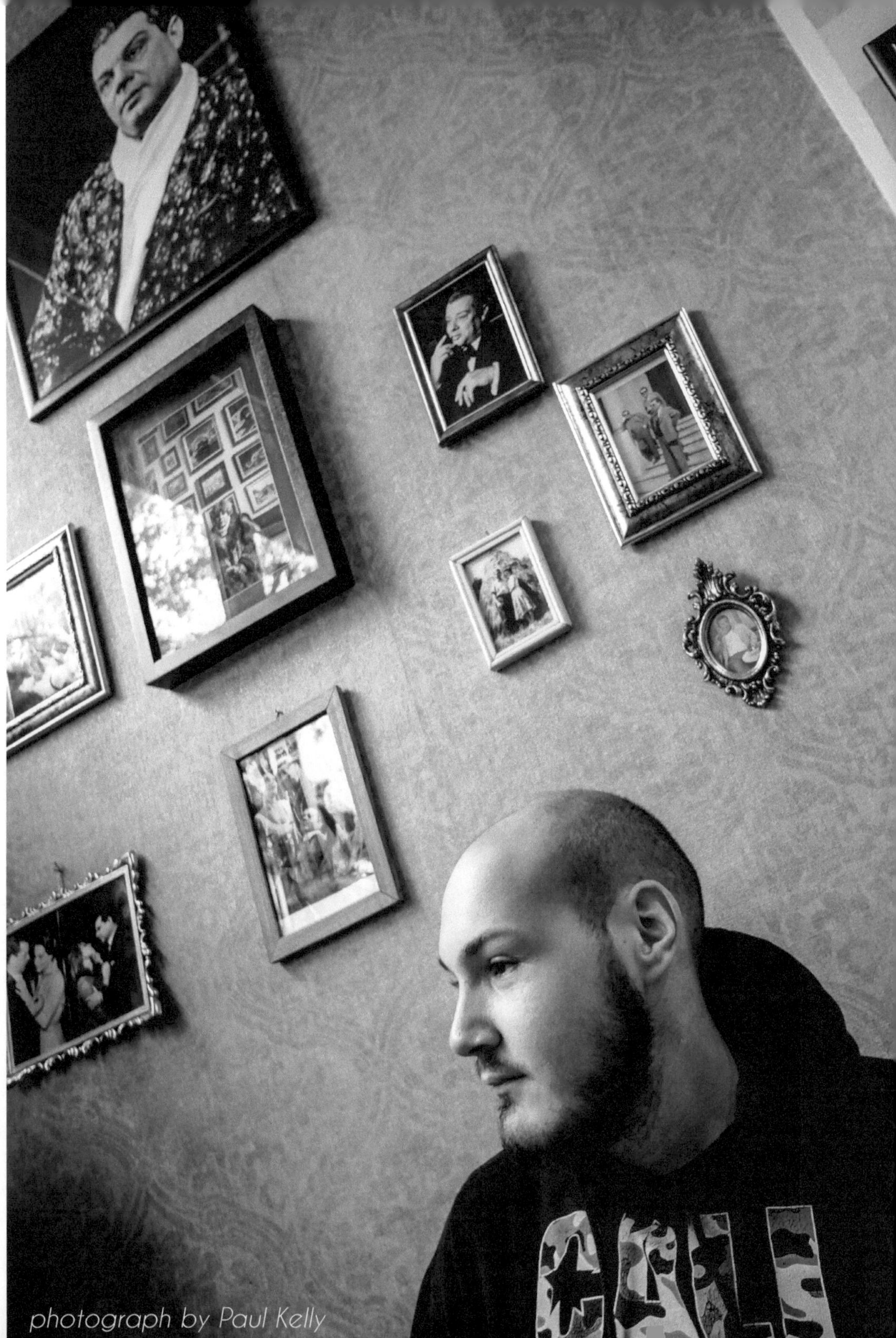

photograph by Paul Kelly

SARAJEVO - Gallery Boris Smoje

Even Goran's staff combine art and caffeine: "I'm an artist and poet who also happens to work here on occasion" says Mernes Zahirović.

photograph by Paul Kelly

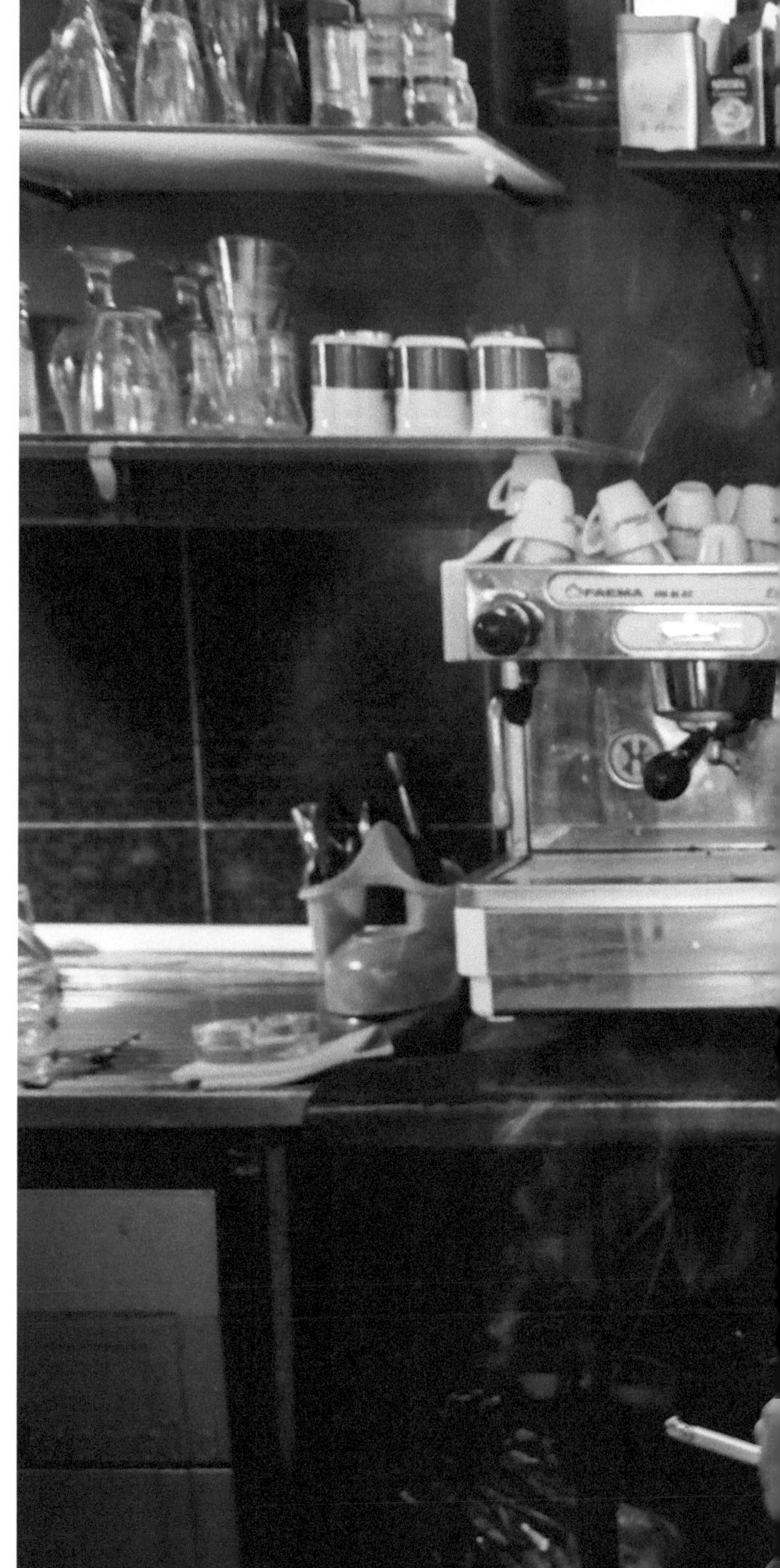

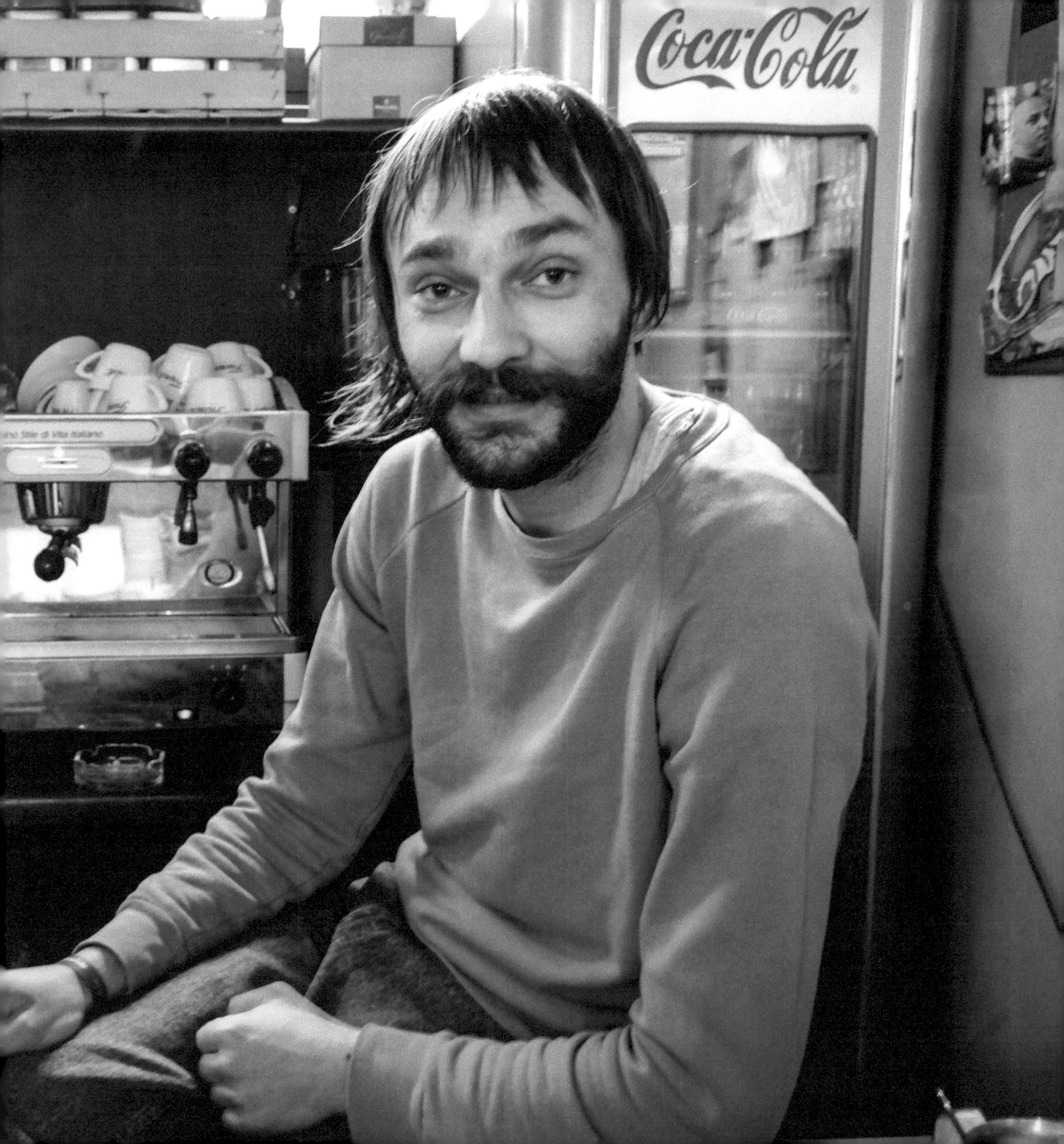
Coca-Cola

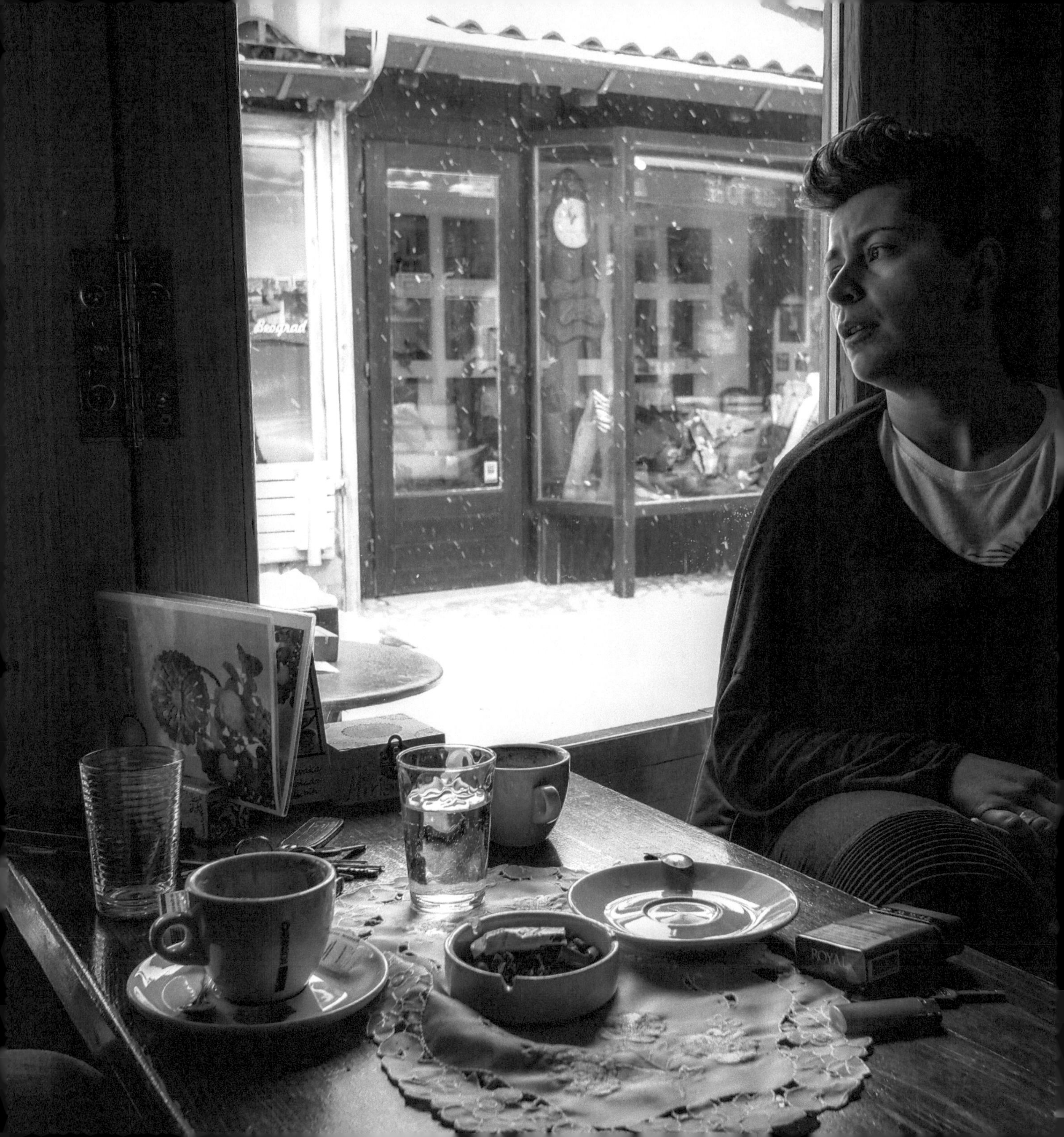
Beograd
ROYAL

SARAJEVO - Café Miras Dunja.

Artist and gallery owner Zana takes a snow-day coffee and smoke break in the Bascarsija quarter of Sarajevo.

photograph by Paul Kelly

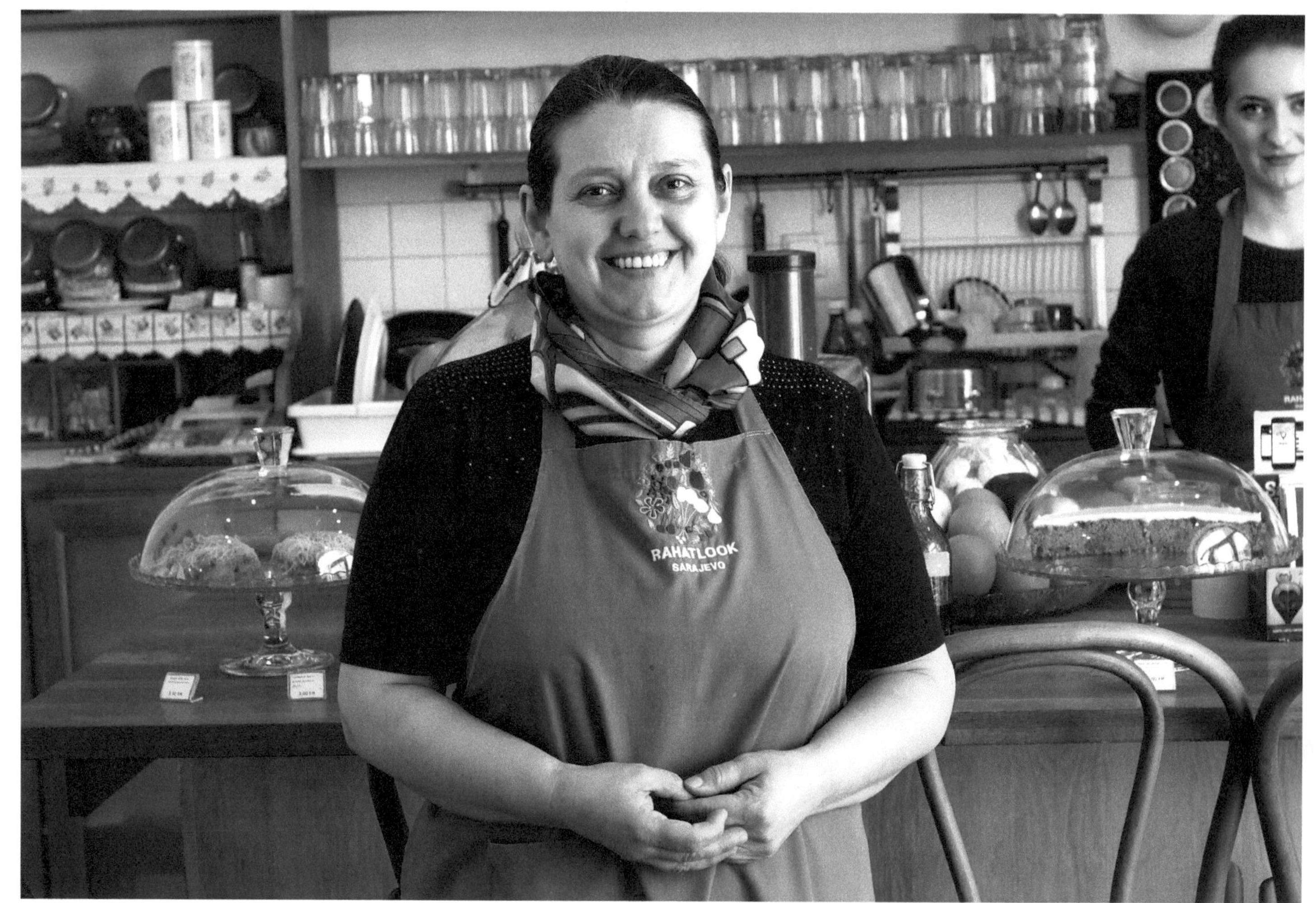

photograph by Fred Shively

SARAJEVO - Rahatlook. In Bosnia and Herzegovina they have an outlook embedded in their genetic code. They say a kind word or smile from a passing stranger, a pleasant thought or memory, a smell or colour, or an encounter with the traditional, may be enough to bring you a moment or more of happiness. This state of mind (and being) is summed up in a Turkish word: rahatluk (pronounced rah-haht-look). For the sake of rahatluk, Snježana Nezirović (smiling, top) decided to give up studying medicine and open her jewel of a café/shop in Sarajevo. Here, she dispenses traditional Bosnian coffee, a taste rainbow of teas, thick hot chocolate, fruit juices and syrups, desserts and baked goods. Of course there was only one name for her café. (right: another customer relishing her daily rahatluk)

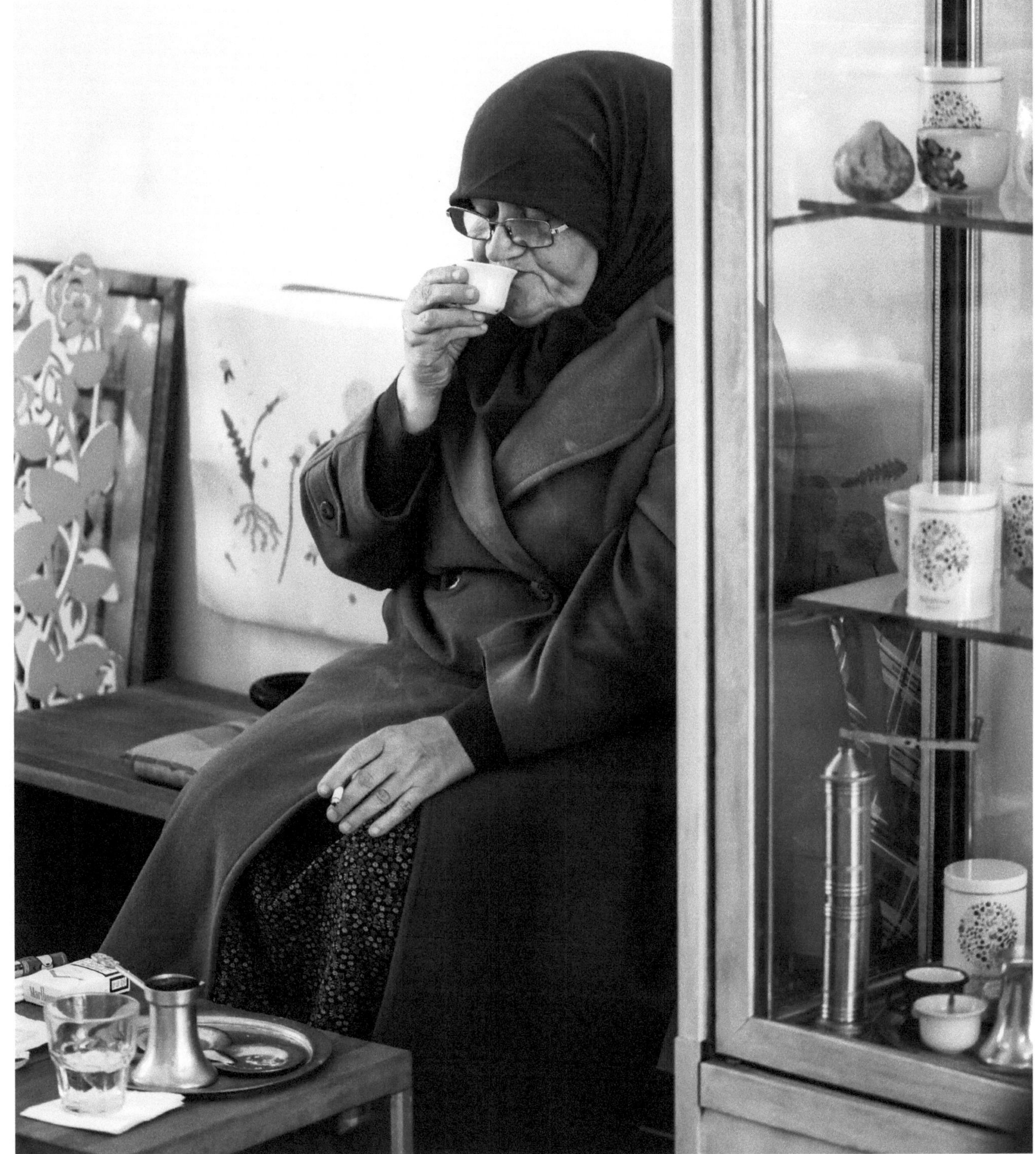

photograph by Paul Kelly

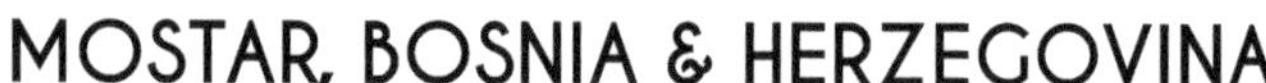

Café de Alma. Jaso Elezovic runs a tiny temple to Bosnian coffee as it should be made and enjoyed. Jaso should know – his family has been roasting, grinding and serving the real thing for generations.

Says Jaso: "this process of making coffee is what I've been taught by my mother who was taught by my grandmother. So it's a family thing. The future is located in the past. We have to go back and take things that were good back then and put them into this world. Then we will be able to define our own culture and identity".

photograph by Paul Kelly

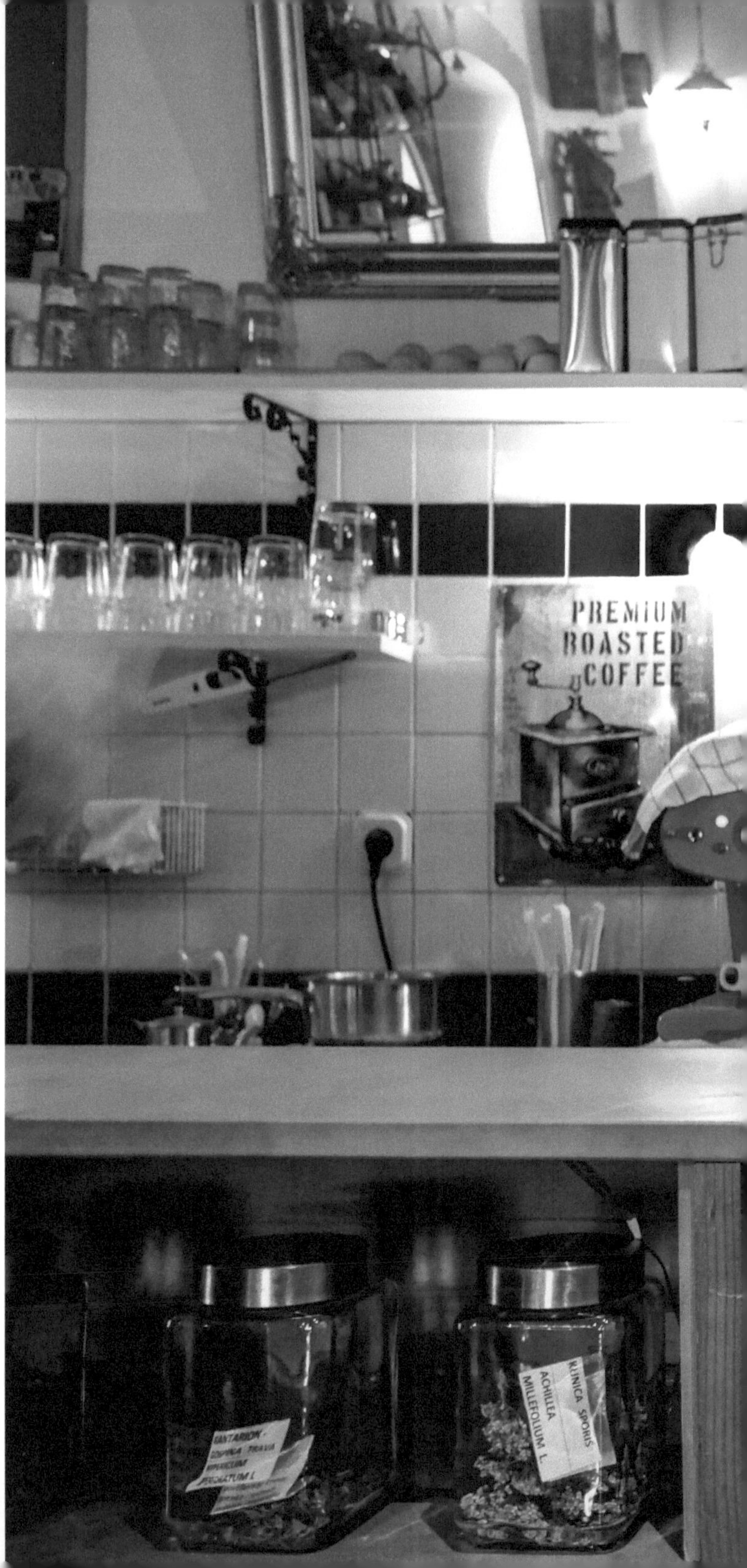

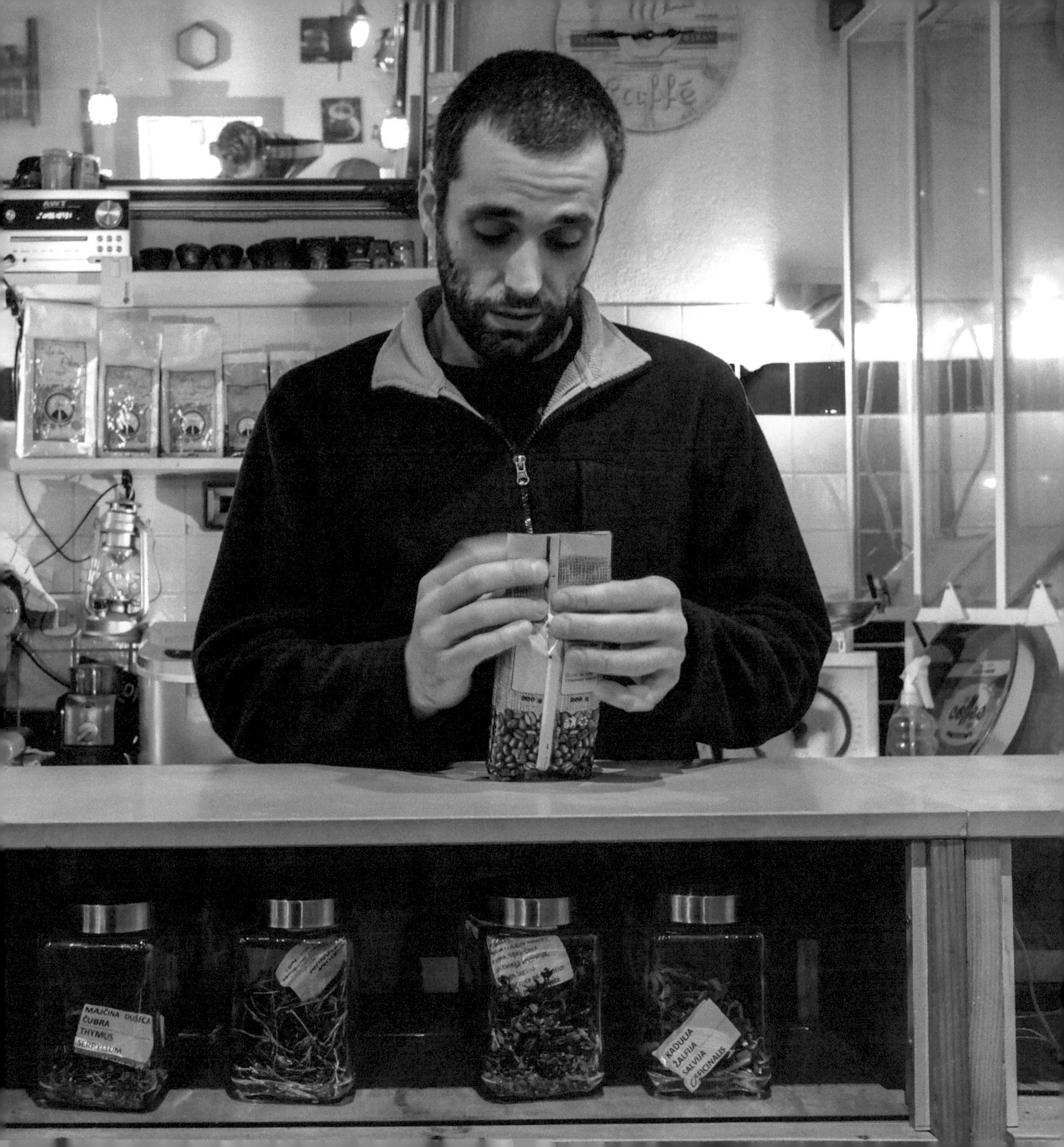
MAJČINA DUŠICA
ČUBRA
THYMUS
SERPYLLUM
KADULJA
ŽALFIJA
SALVIJA
OFFICINALIS

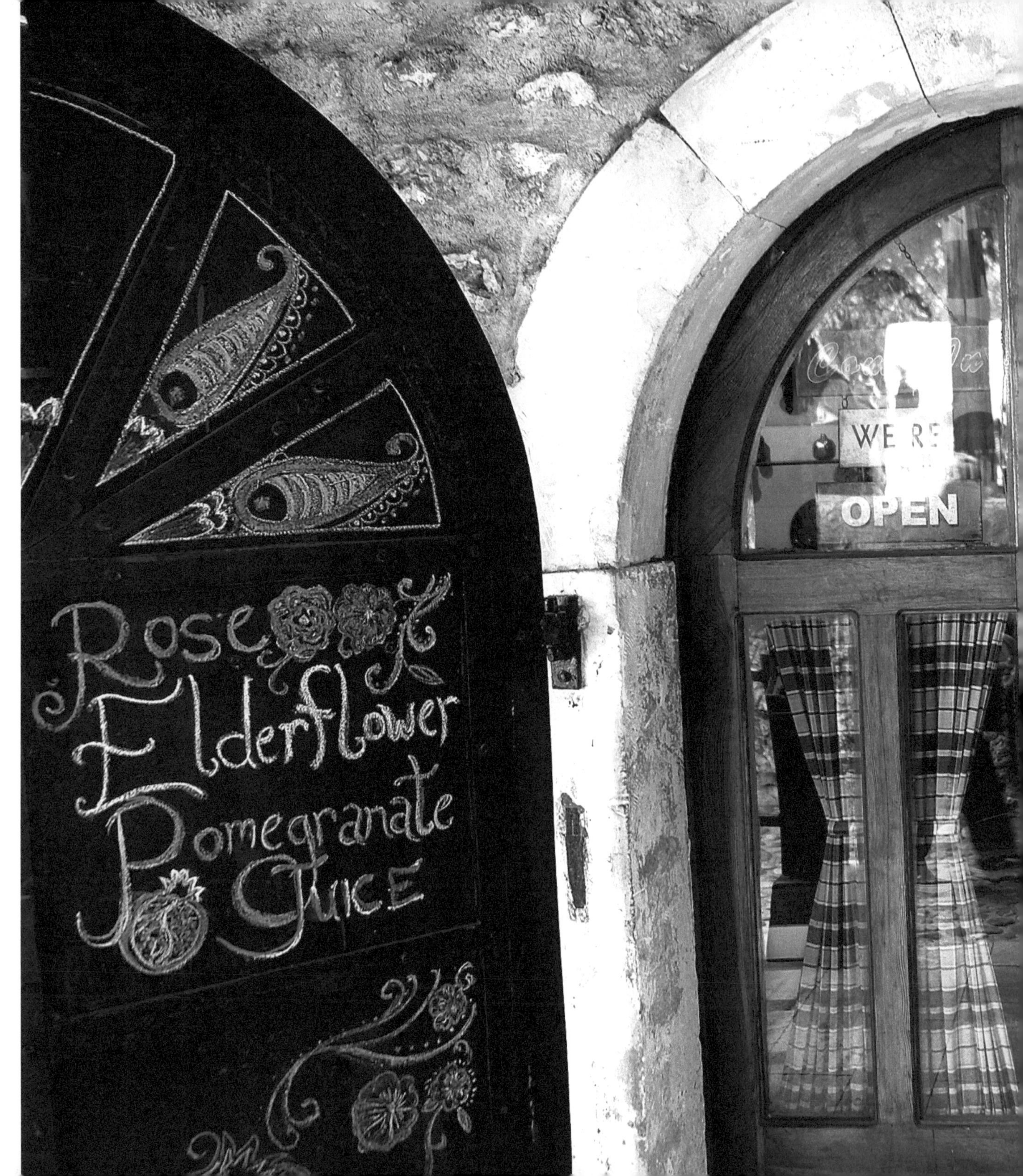
Rose
Elderflower
Pomegranate
Juice
WE'RE
OPEN

photograph by Fred Shively

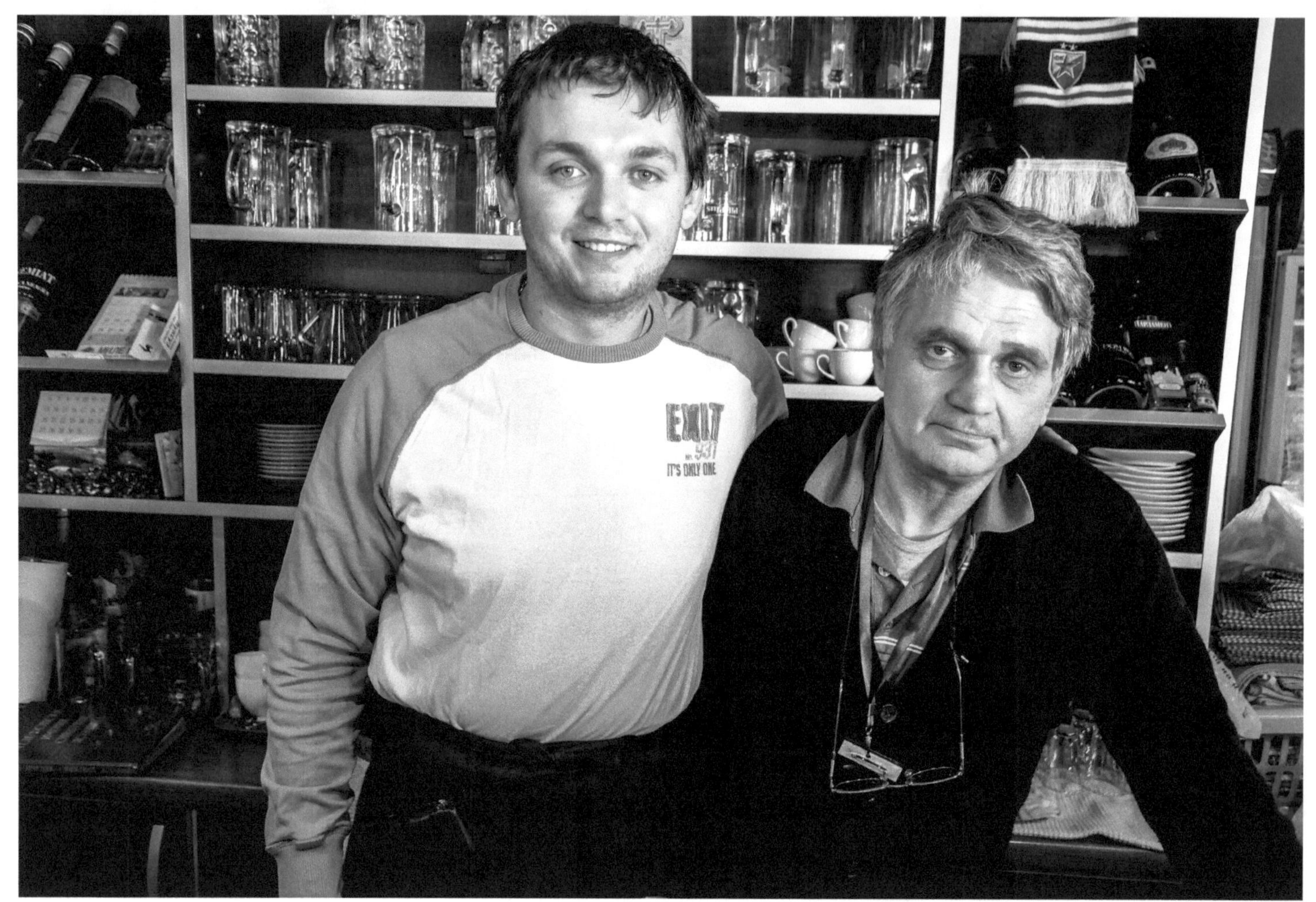

photograph by Paul Kelly

LOZNICA, SERBIA – café/bar Stirske Véceri. Dragan Despopović (above with his son Miloš) has owned and operated this typical working man's coffee, beer and rakia café/bar for 30 years. Food isn't served and women don't tend to visit. If you order a 'married coffee' you'll get a cup of black coffee with a shot of rakia on the side. Dragan says about 40% of his customers "are the marrying type".

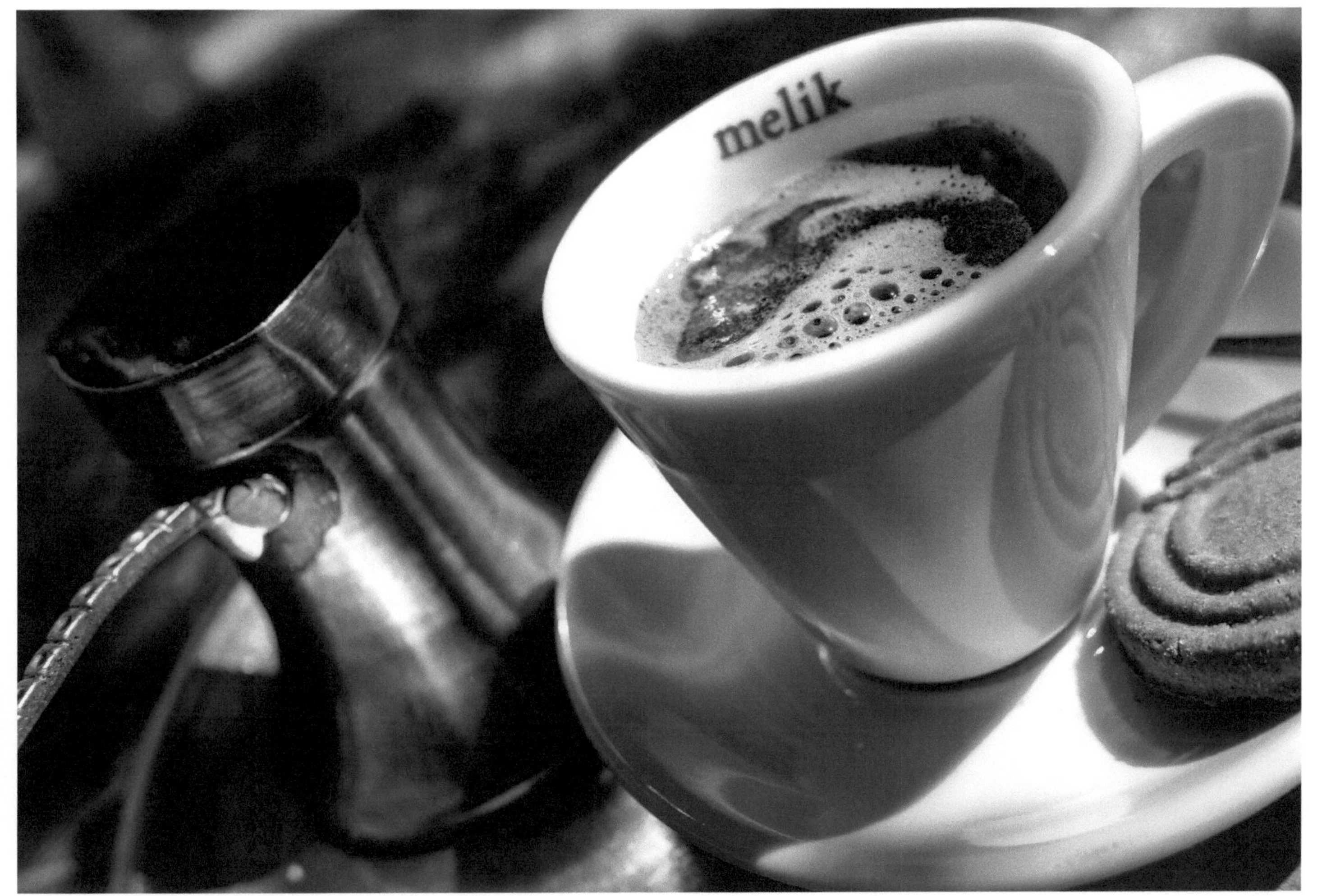

photograph by Paul Kelly

SERBIA – 'docekusa, rozgovarusa, sikterusa'. In Serbia, these words mean the welcoming first coffee, the conversational second cup and the 'shoo' or 'time-you-were-going' third cup. It's sometimes known as the three coffee rule. You are a special guest or friend indeed if you make it through all three.

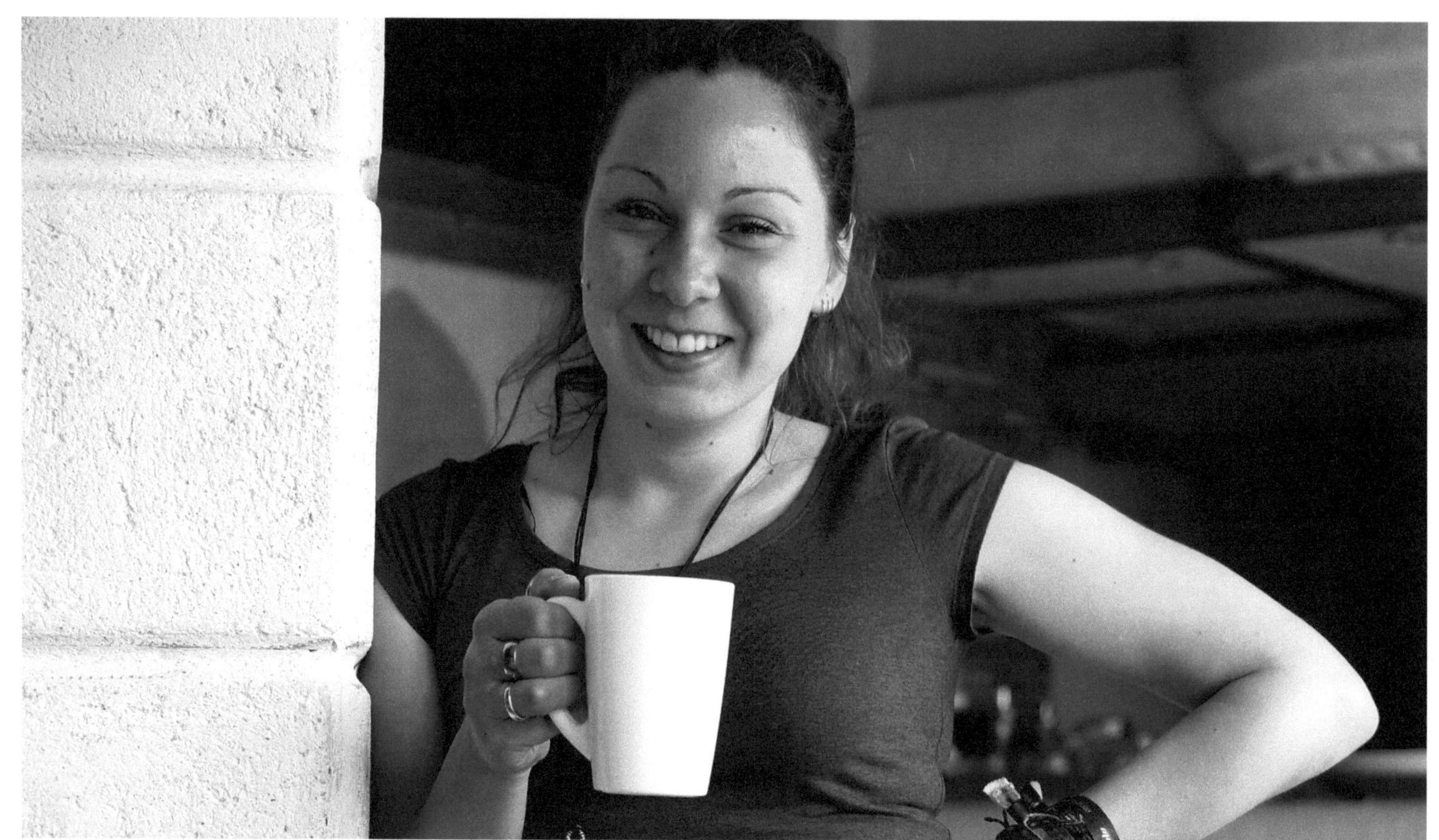

photograph by Fred Shively

BELGRADE, SERBIA – Beogradski Pobednik Kafe. Hidden in the grounds of the Citadel of Belgrade this is a favourite haunt of students. Manageress Vana (above) says, "I don't like coffee...it's so addictive!" But she also says, "when I don't drink coffee I don't know where I am"

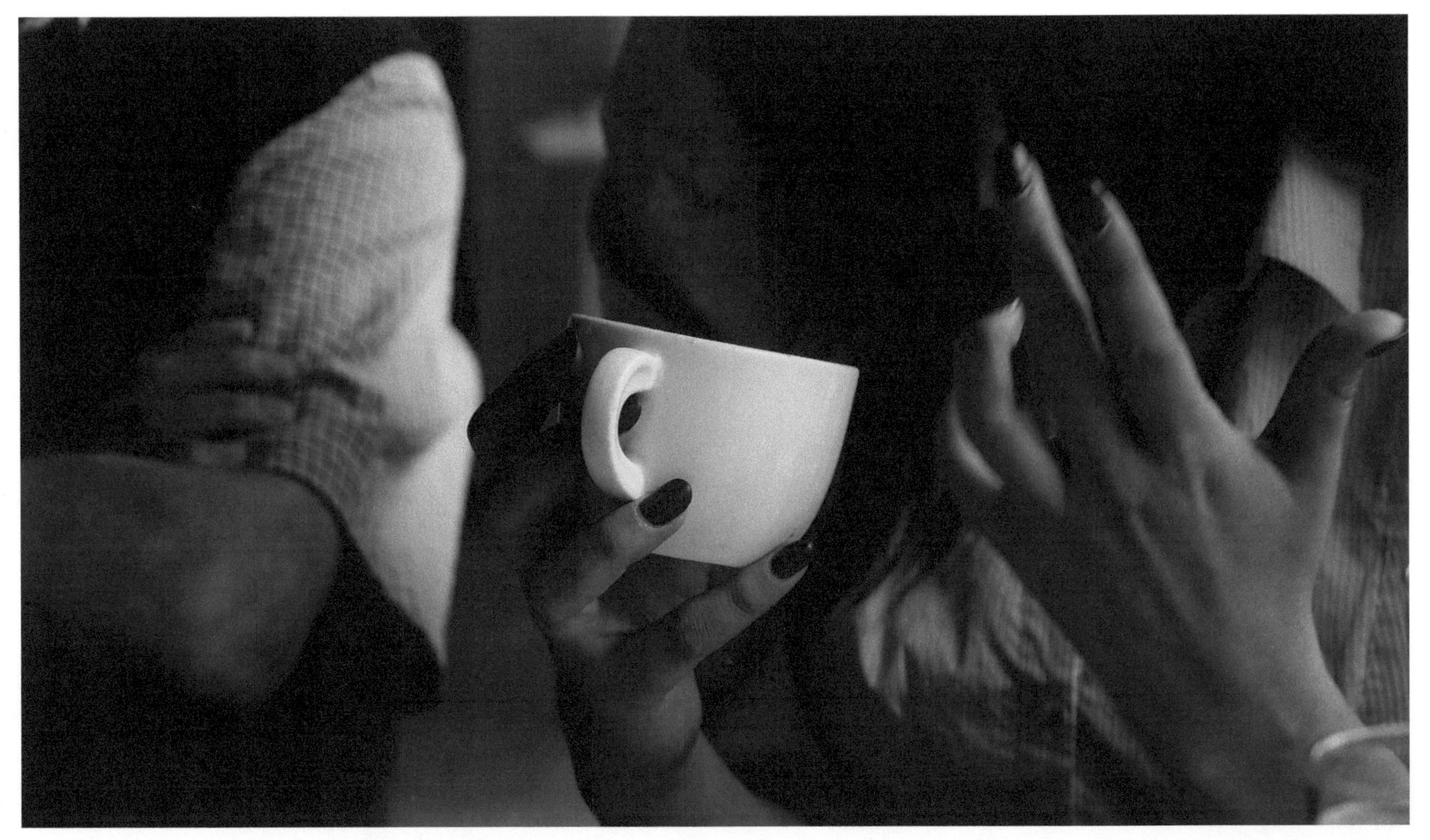

photograph by Fred Shively

BELGRADE - Another Serbian coffee tradition: the reading of the coffee grounds. At Beogradski Pobednik Kafe, manager Ivana was to be our foreteller, but an influx of customers took her away. So Kristina, our guide, takes over, finding fascination in the silted remains.

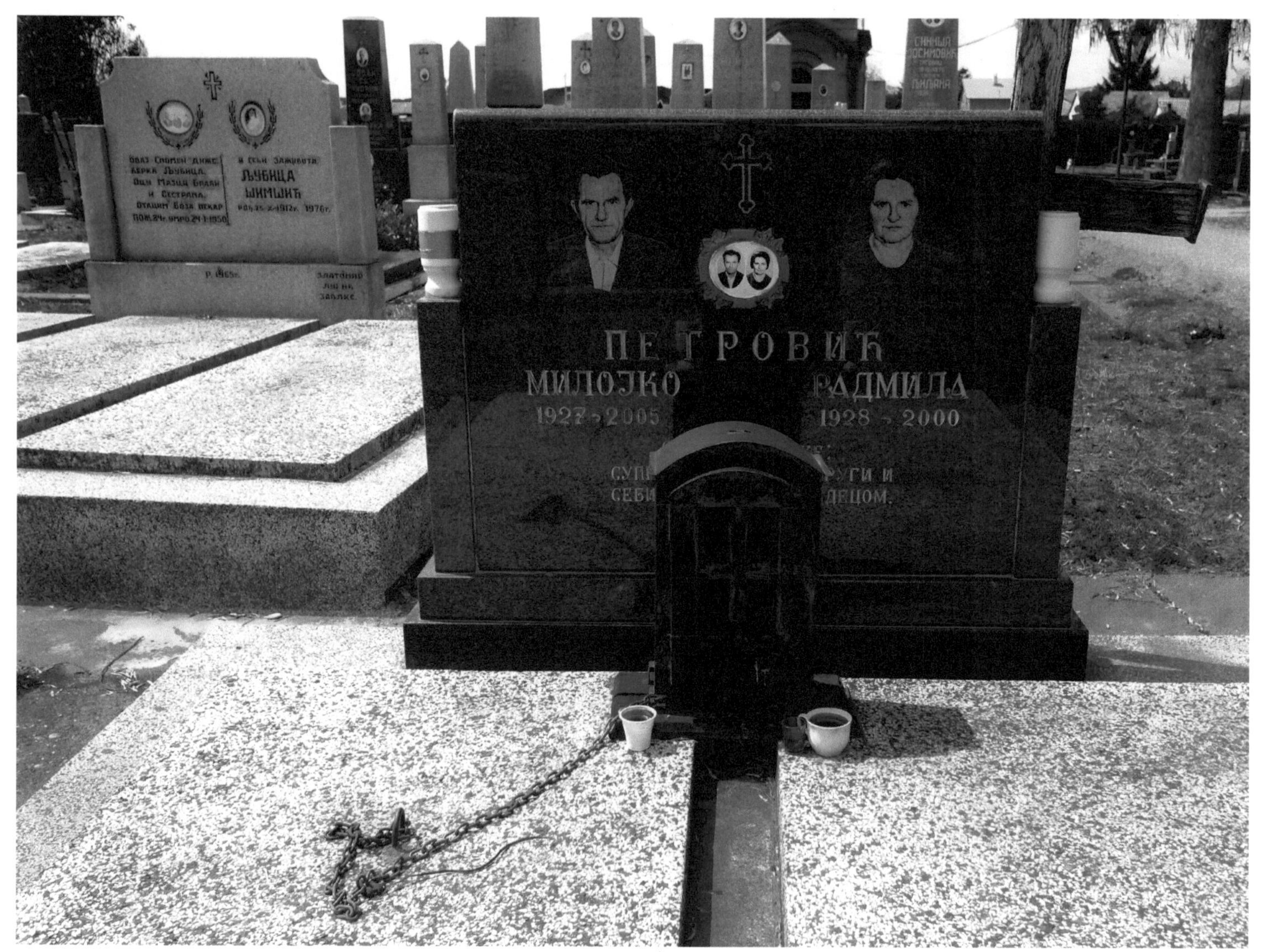

photograph by Paul Kelly

LOZNICA - Kristina assembles what she needs: chocolate, an apple, thermos of good Serbian coffee, two cups and several thin candles. She's off to visit her uncle and we're going along – no matter that uncle has been dead for over 20 years. Kristina lights the candles, places chocolate and an apple at the grave and pours coffee into two cups. Now Kristina places one cup near the headstone, sips her own coffee, and settles down for a good gossip.

NOVI SAD, SERBIA - Several years ago Maja Gredić lost her job as a marketing executive and knew exactly what she had to do with her life. "I had travelled the world for work and always loved the taste of good coffee," she explained. "In Serbia, I didn't find coffee that tasted as good. And I believe that the true mark of your country's quality is reflected in the quality of your coffee." Back from her travels, Maja opened a small coffee kiosk in Novi Sad. At Barka Kafa, Maja roasts all her coffee at home, then grinds and packages the beans at her shop. On each brown paper coffee bag, Maja handwrites personal notes: "You are the coffee you drink" and "With a cup of coffee, even a day in Serbia has some chance."

photograph by Paul Kelly

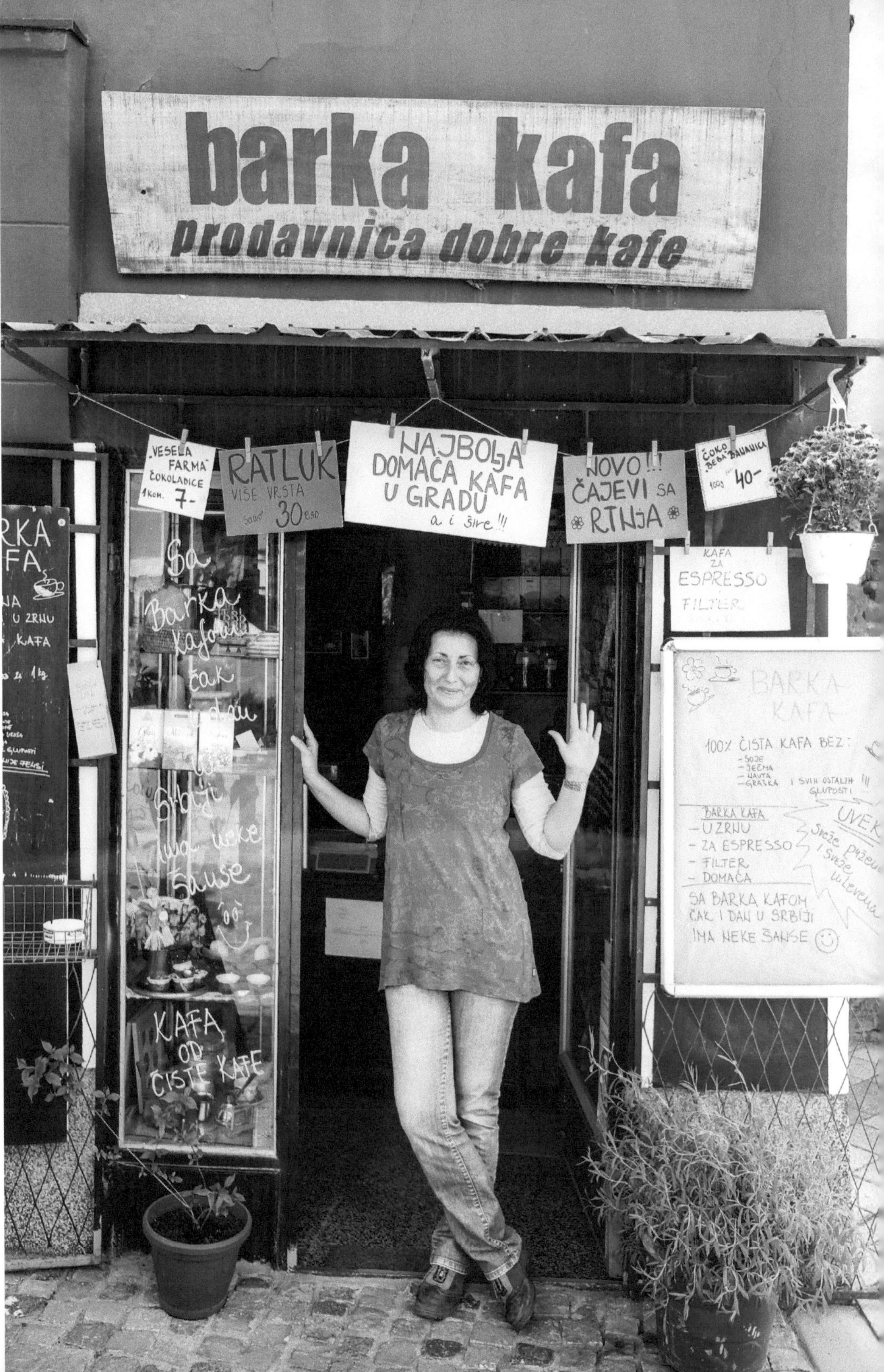

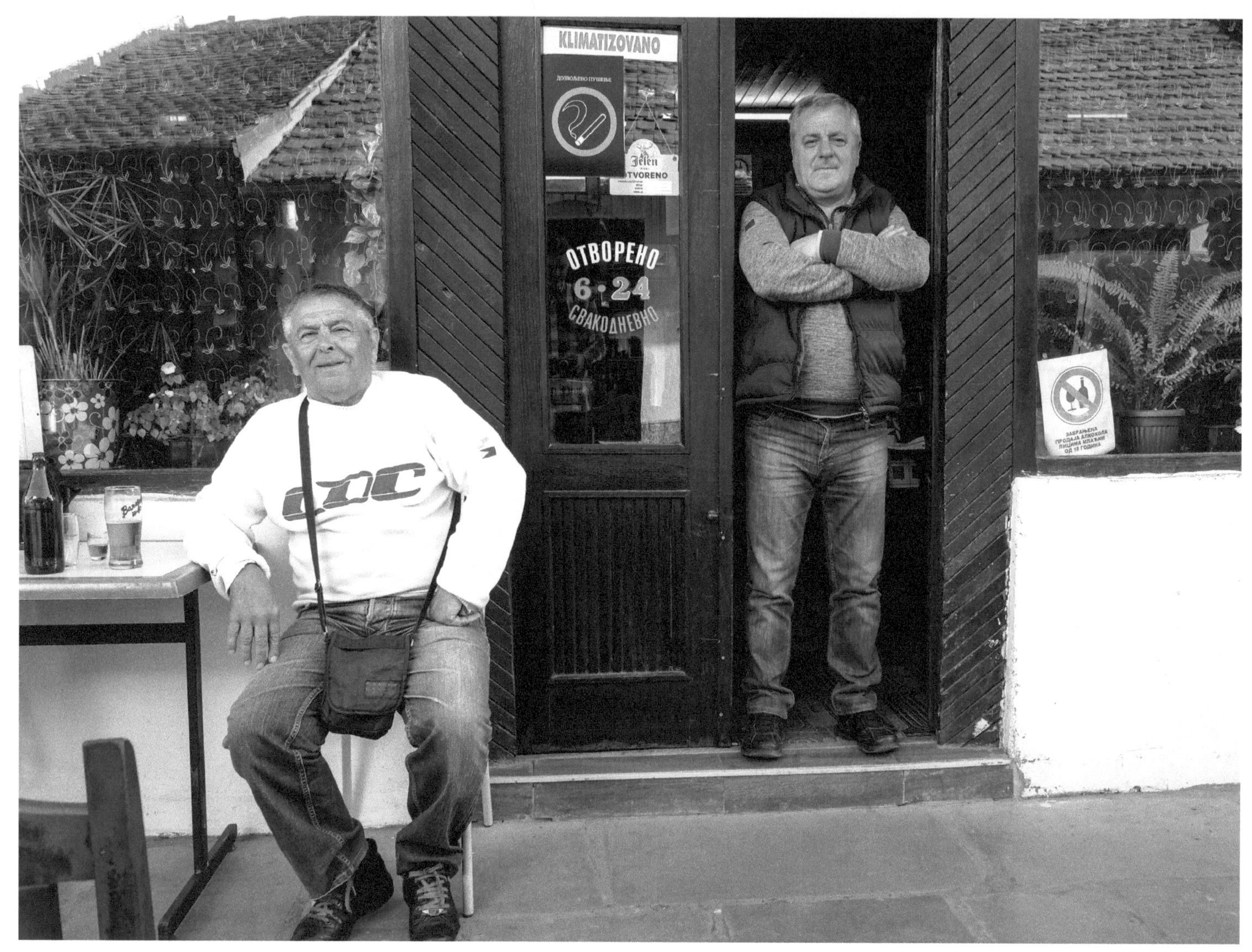

photograph by Paul Kelly

VALJEVO, SERBIA - In Serbia kafanas , small neighbourhood café/bars proliferate. It's where the locals meet, socialize over coffee, beer, the ubiquitous, potent rakia, and play cards and dominoes. Such a place is Kod Bore in Valjevo. Says proprietor Borivoje Dragojevic (Bore for short, in the doorway), "you enter a kafana alone and you leave with three godfathers".

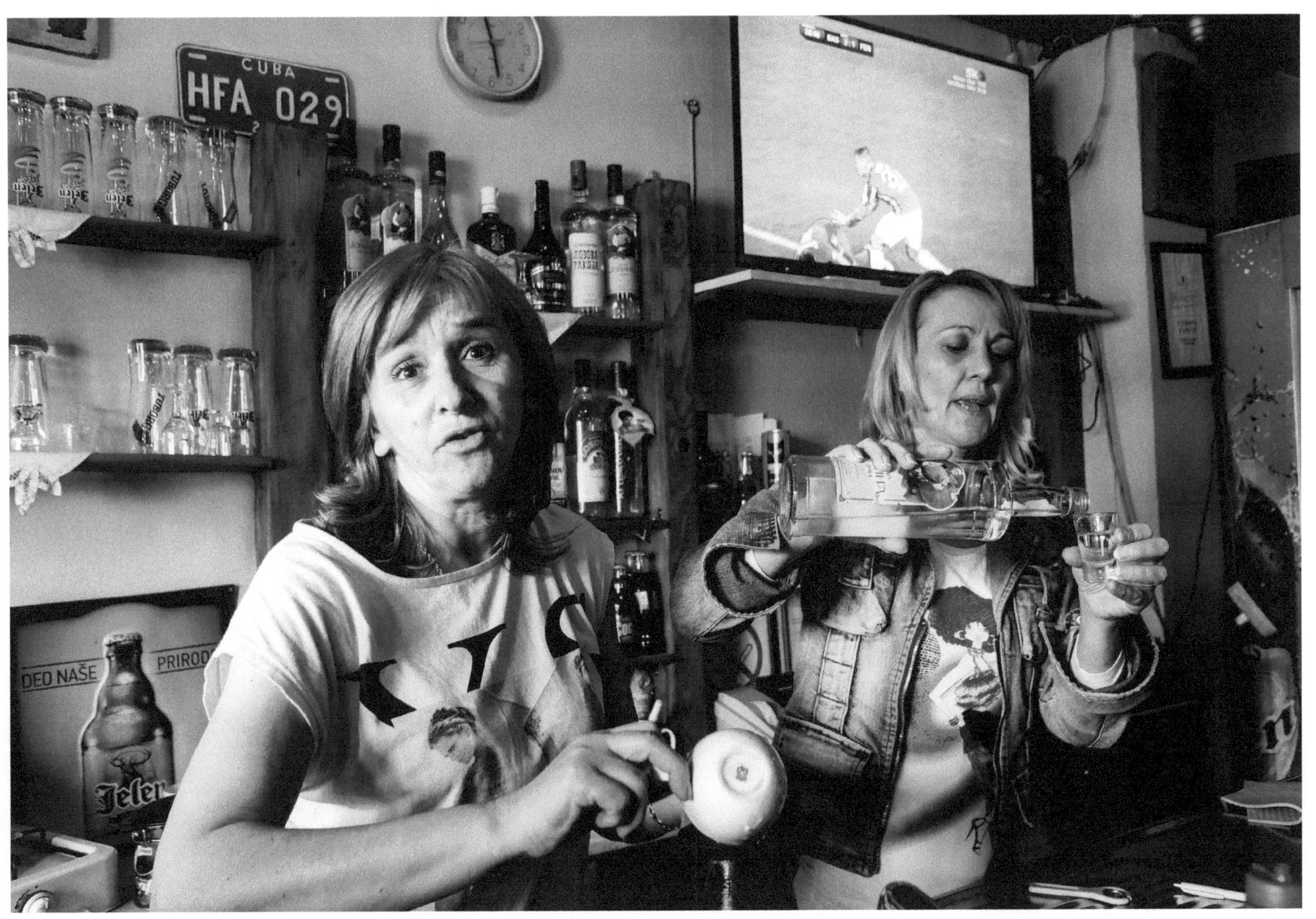

photograph by Paul Kelly

NOVI SAD - Cep Bar. Aside from great hosts there are four key ingredients for a 'good' neighbourhood café/bar in Serbia: coffee, beer, rakia and a football match on the telly.

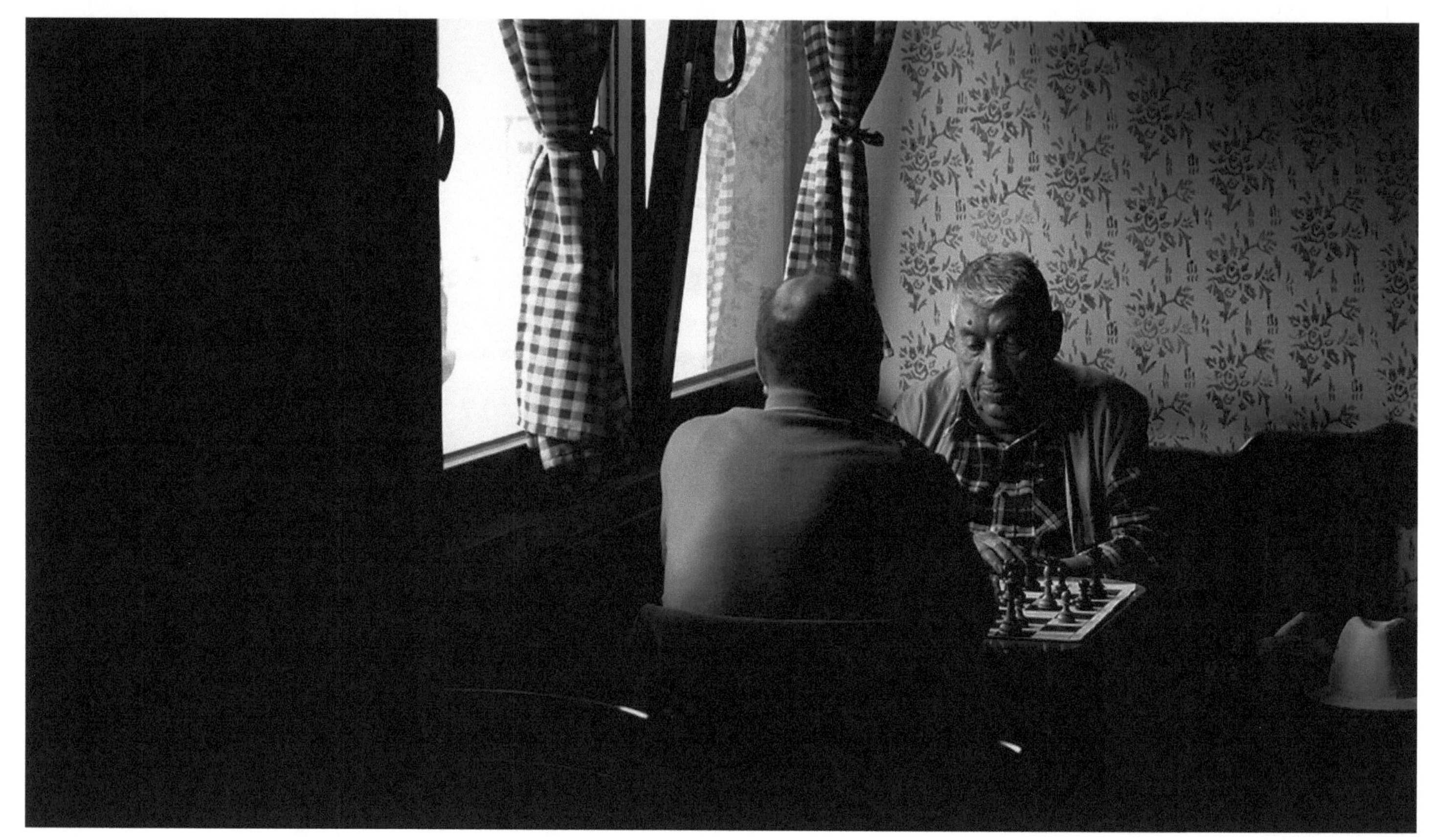

photograph by Fred Shively

NOVI SAD - Kafana Rujna Zora. Kafanas in Serbia are often hotbeds of intensive chess playing.

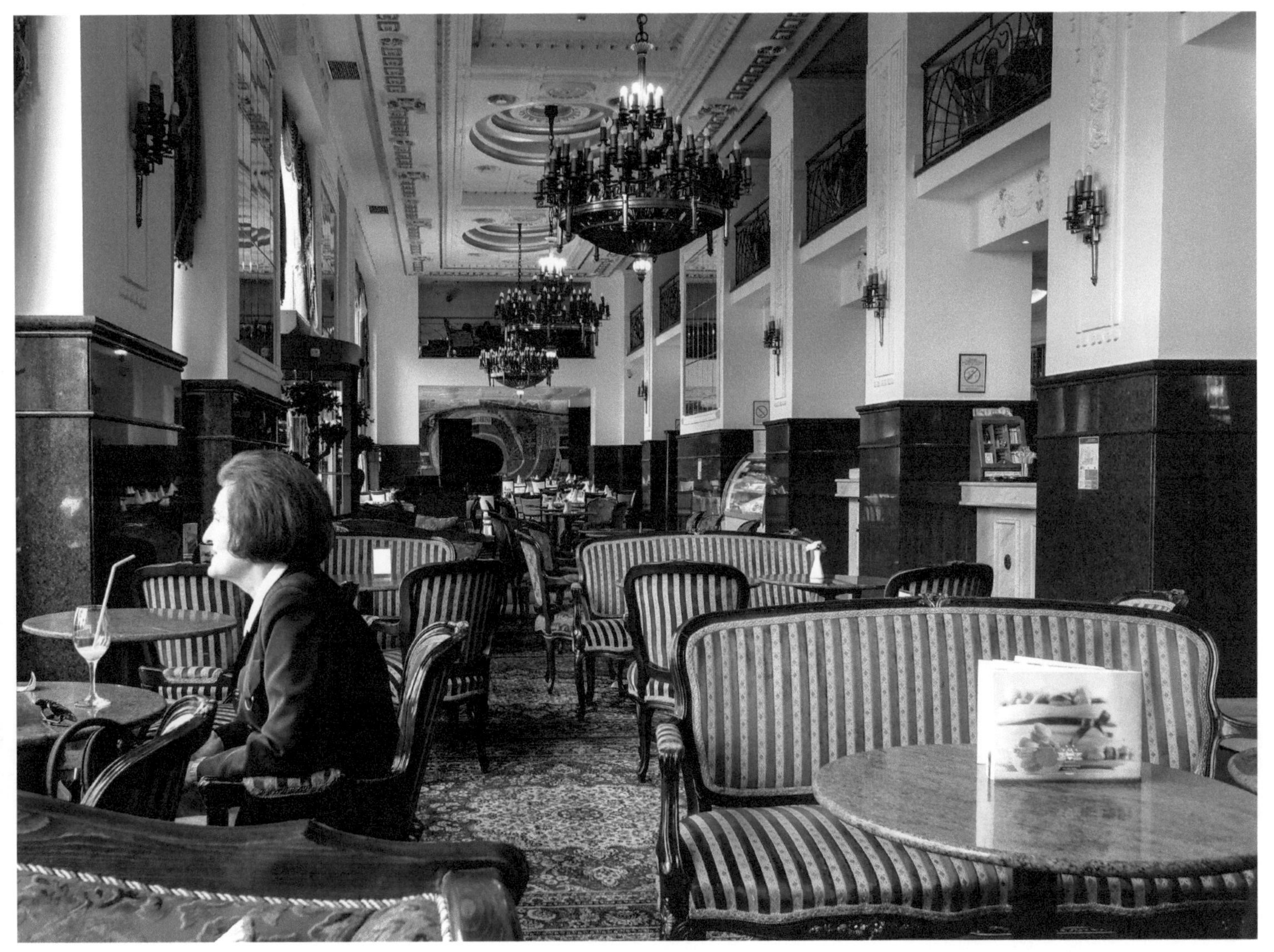

photograph by Paul Kelly

BELGRADE - From single storey house at the turn of the 20th century, to Russian insurance company HQ in 1908, the Hotel Moskva in Belgrade - and its grand café - have changed with the times. Says Milka (90), one of its most loyal patrons: "despite all the hardships - World War II, Communism, Milosevic, the 1999 bombings - we still have time for our coffee, don't we?"

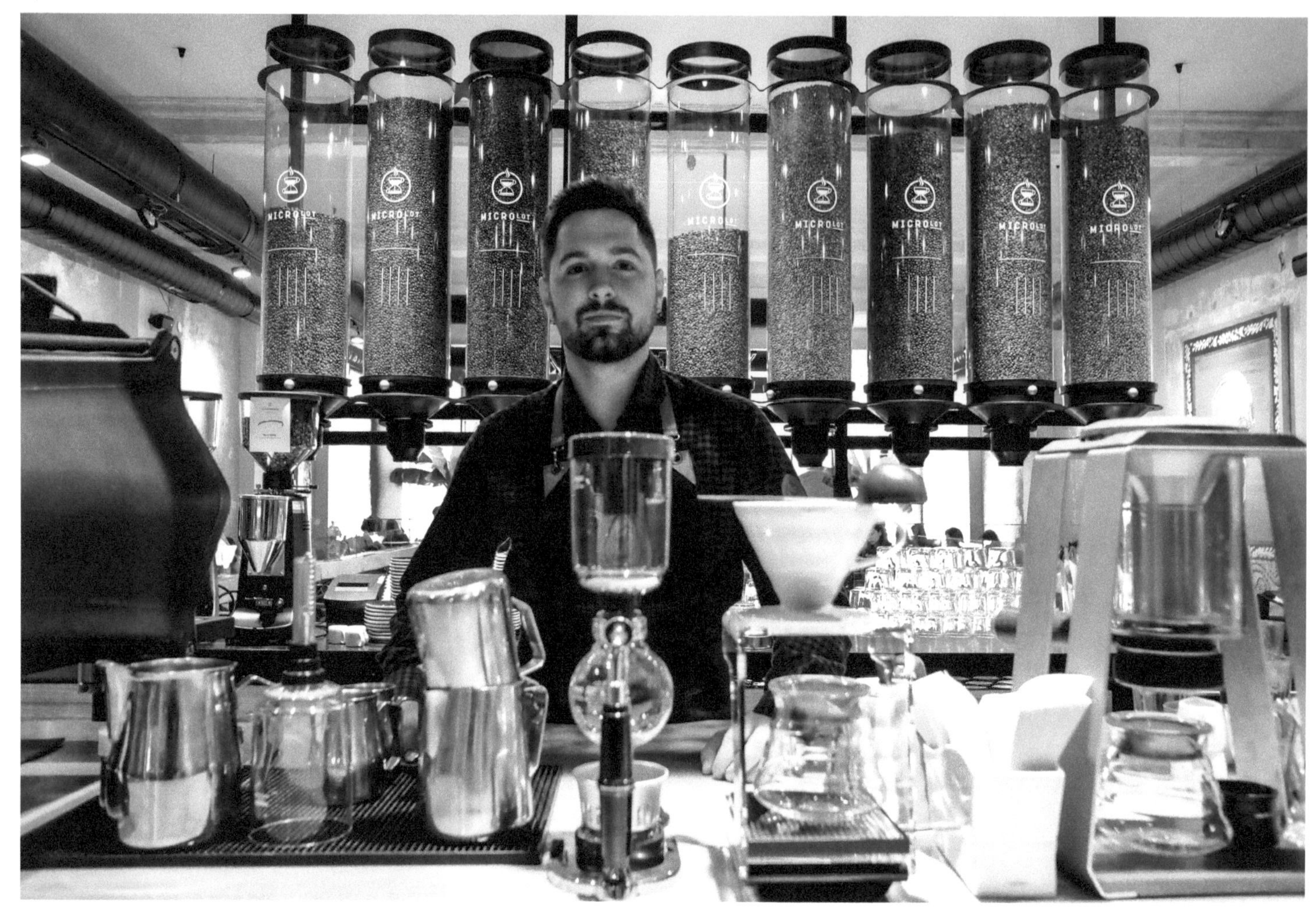

photograph by Paul Kelly

BELGRADE – Kafeterija. “Traditional cafés have their own sparkle, but this café is the new way. It’s a more creative, more challenging environment to me as an artist. Tradition doesn’t challenge me.” So says Zaneseni Umetnik, head barista at Kafeterija. The three-storey, industrial-modern venue is one of the new breed of coffee dispensaries making their mark in Belgrade.

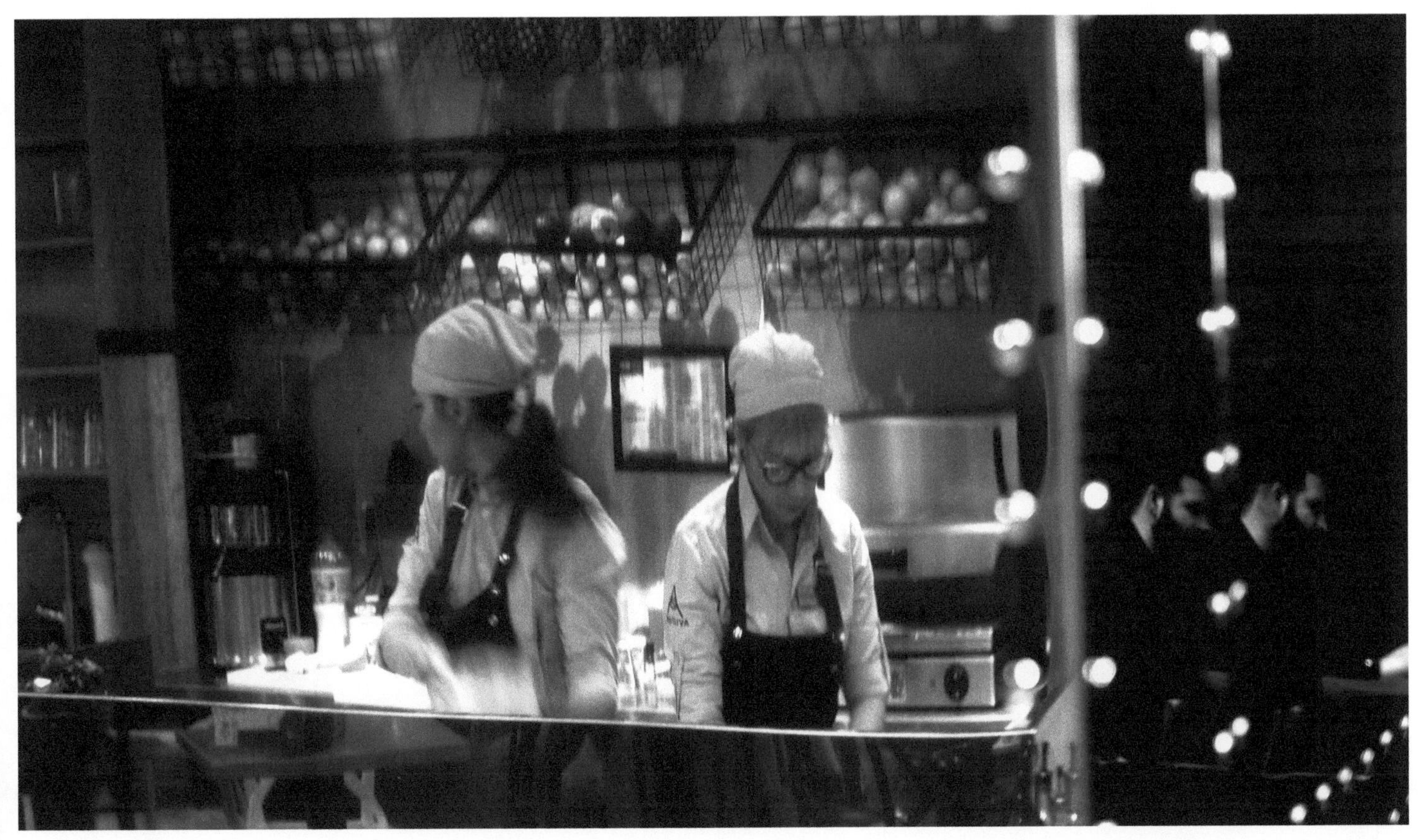

photograph by Fred Shively

BELGRADE – Aviator. The future of café culture in Belgrade. As the younger generation indulges its taste for third wave coffees and socializing, sleek, modern venues are showing the way. Along with Kafeterija (previous page), Aviator (above) is a prime example.

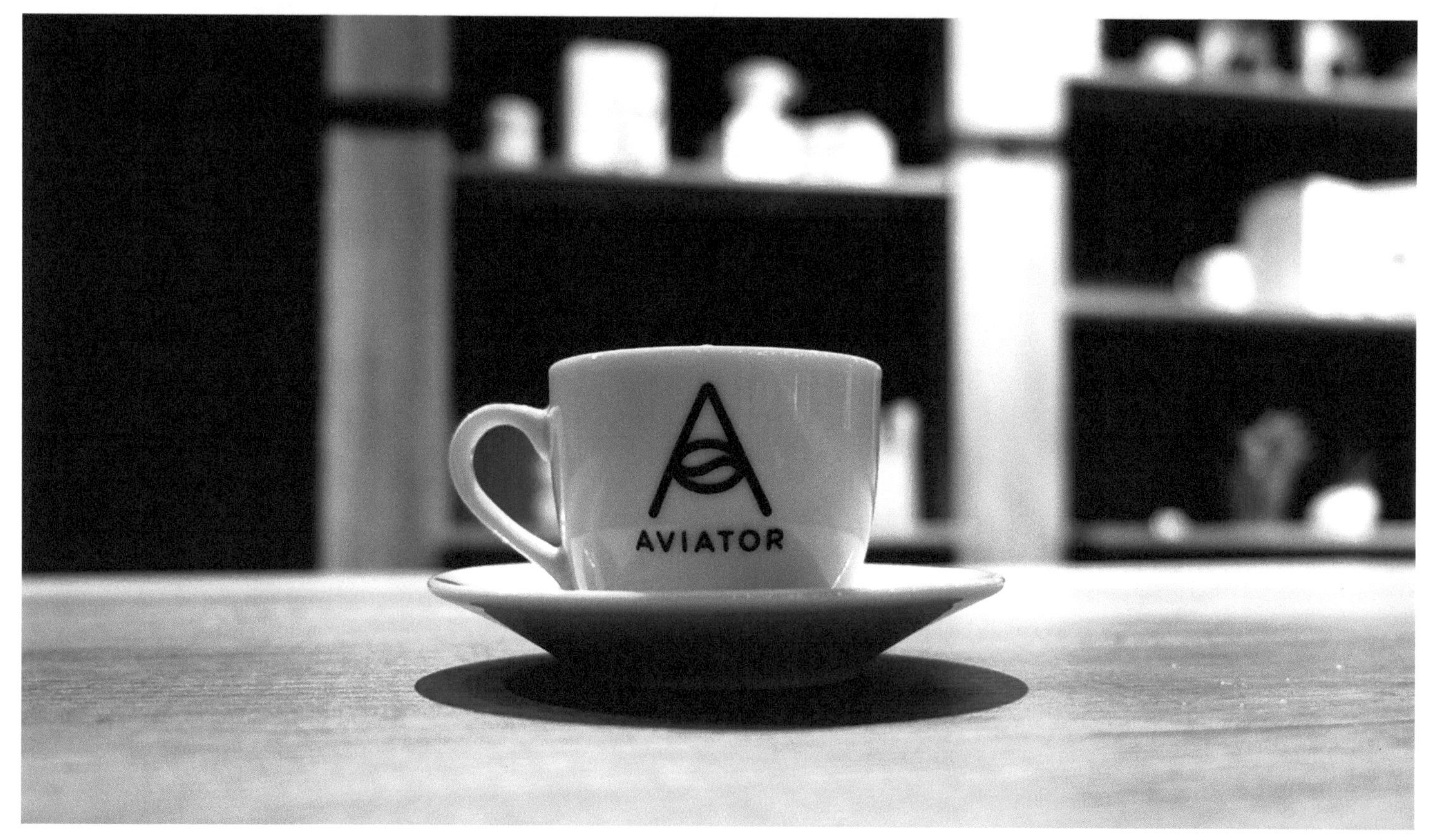

photograph by Fred Shively

BELGRADE – Aviator. The object of young consumer desire in Belgrade: new wave coffee in new wave surroundings.

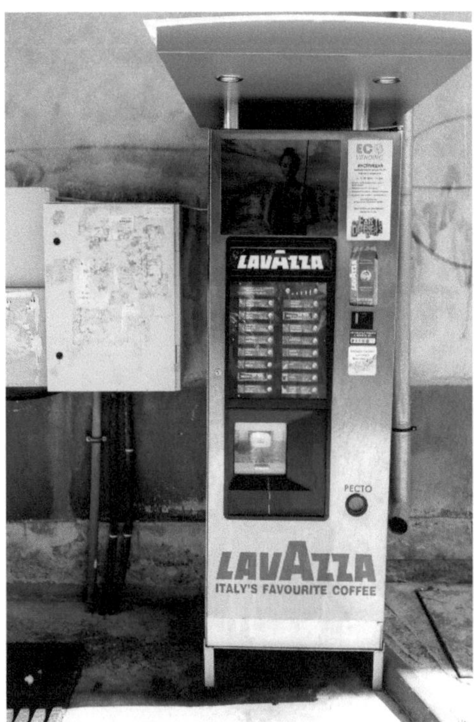

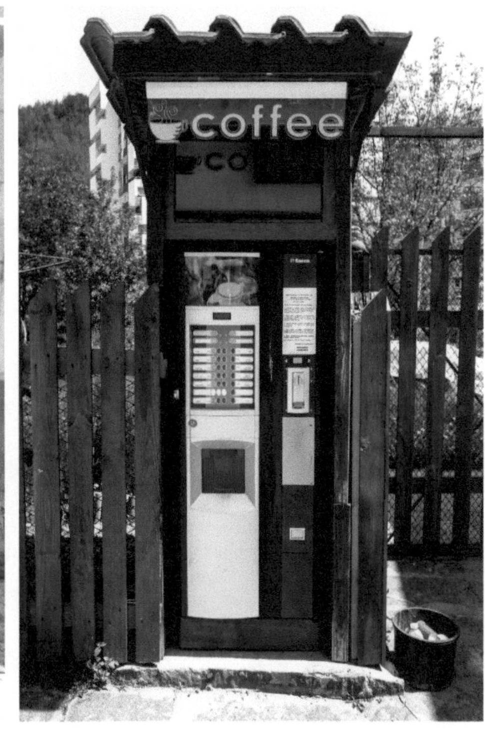

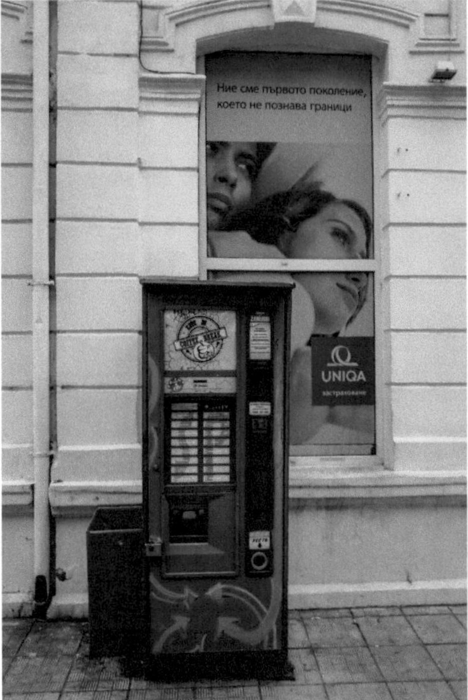

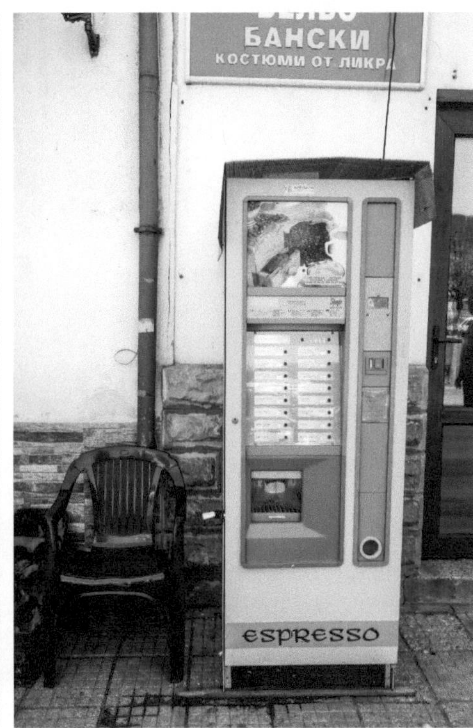

BULGARIA - In Bulgaria we found almost as many, if not more, coffee vending machines as cafés. Apparently a legacy of the communist regime, when people were afraid to socialise in public.

photograph by Paul Kelly

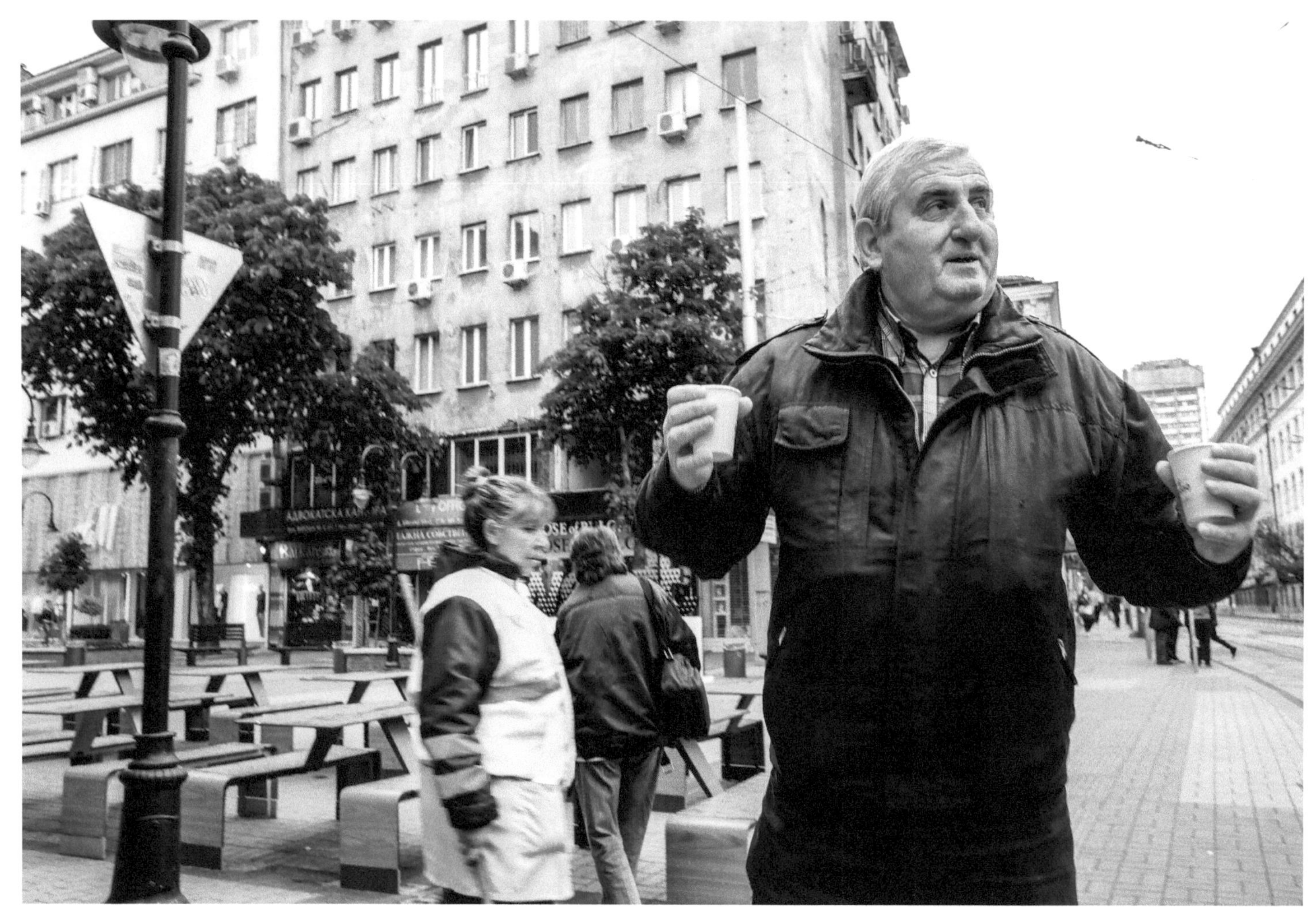

photograph by Paul Kelly

SOFIA, BULGARIA - Coffee on the run - a feature of Bulgarian coffee culture: coffee vending machines vs. cafés. The machines seem to be winning.

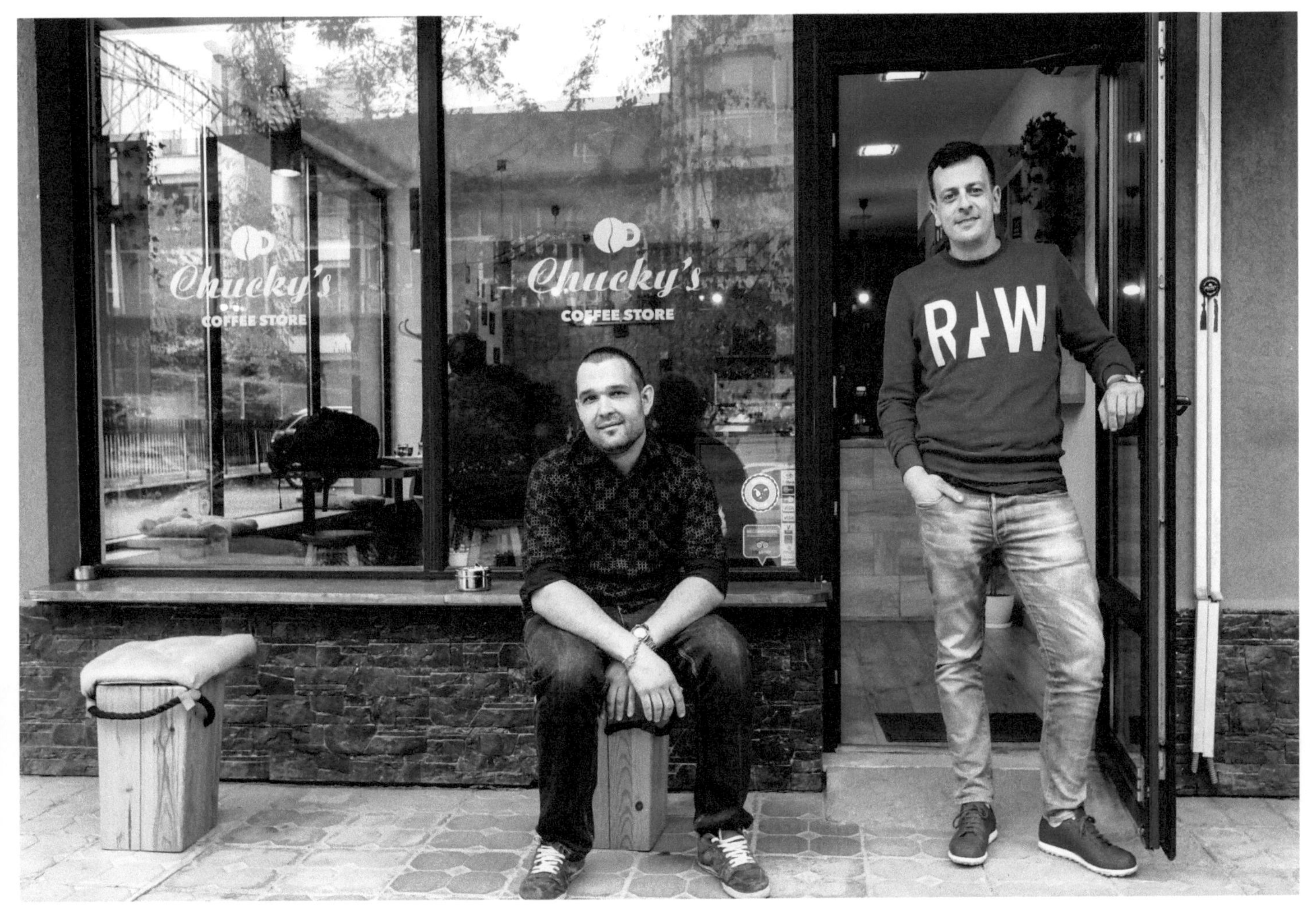

photograph by Paul Kelly

SOFIA - Chucky's Coffee & Culture. The revolution against Bulgaria's indifferent café culture starts here in Sofia. While most of the city's residents have yet to wake up to this brave new world, Dimo Kolev and Ivan Chavdarov go full steam ahead with their two locations and a lot of optimism. Chucky's claims to be the first specialty café in Sofia.

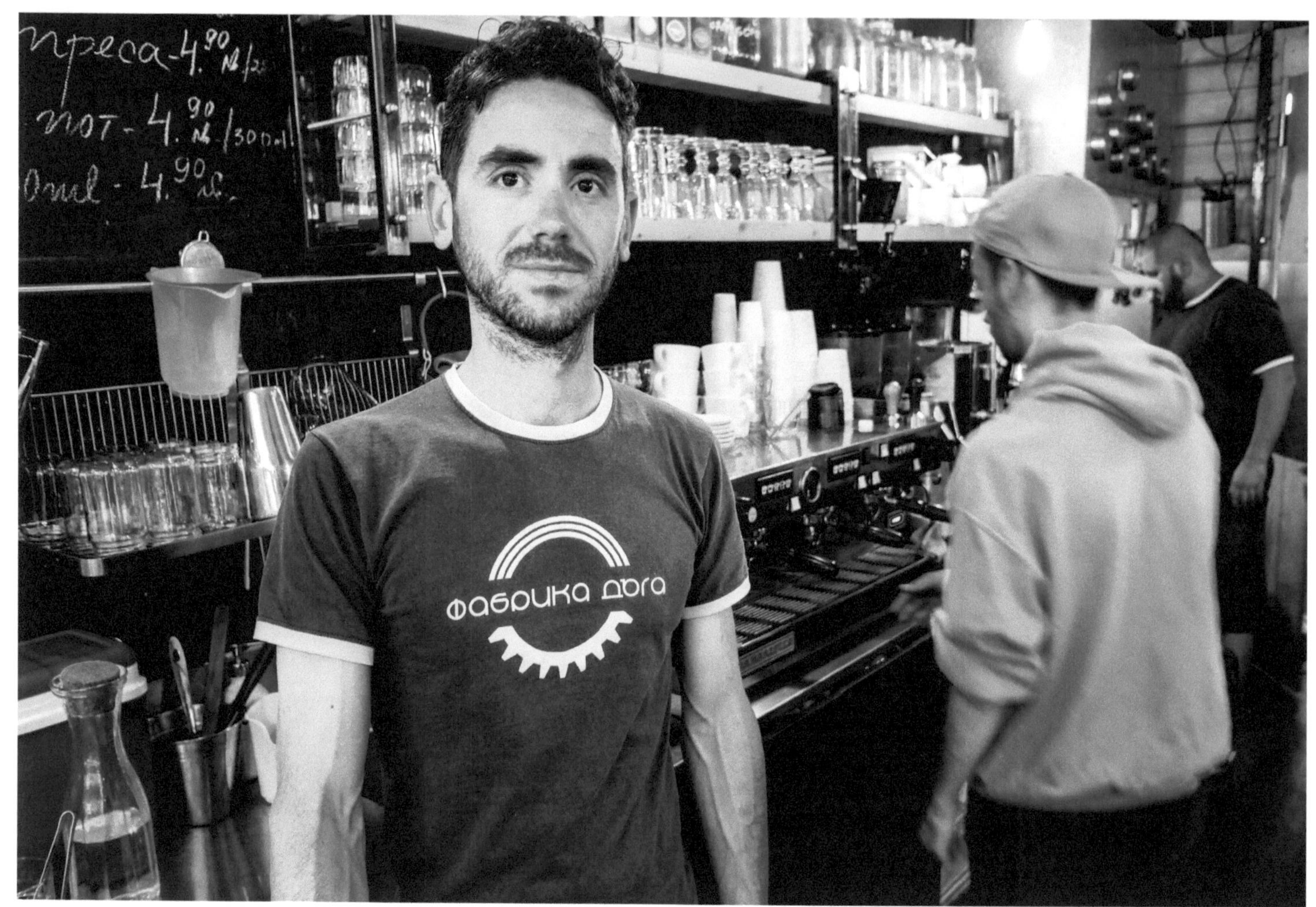

photograph by Paul Kelly

SOFIA - Fabrika Daga. Café owner/barista Venelin Dimitrov: "Fabrika Daga has been open for three years. People come here for the coffee and social scene. People here in Sofia can't afford a lot of coffee, can't afford to go to the cafés all the time. So the coffee has to be good. If you don't serve good coffee your business is doomed. Also tourism plays an important role. As tourism grows so will we."

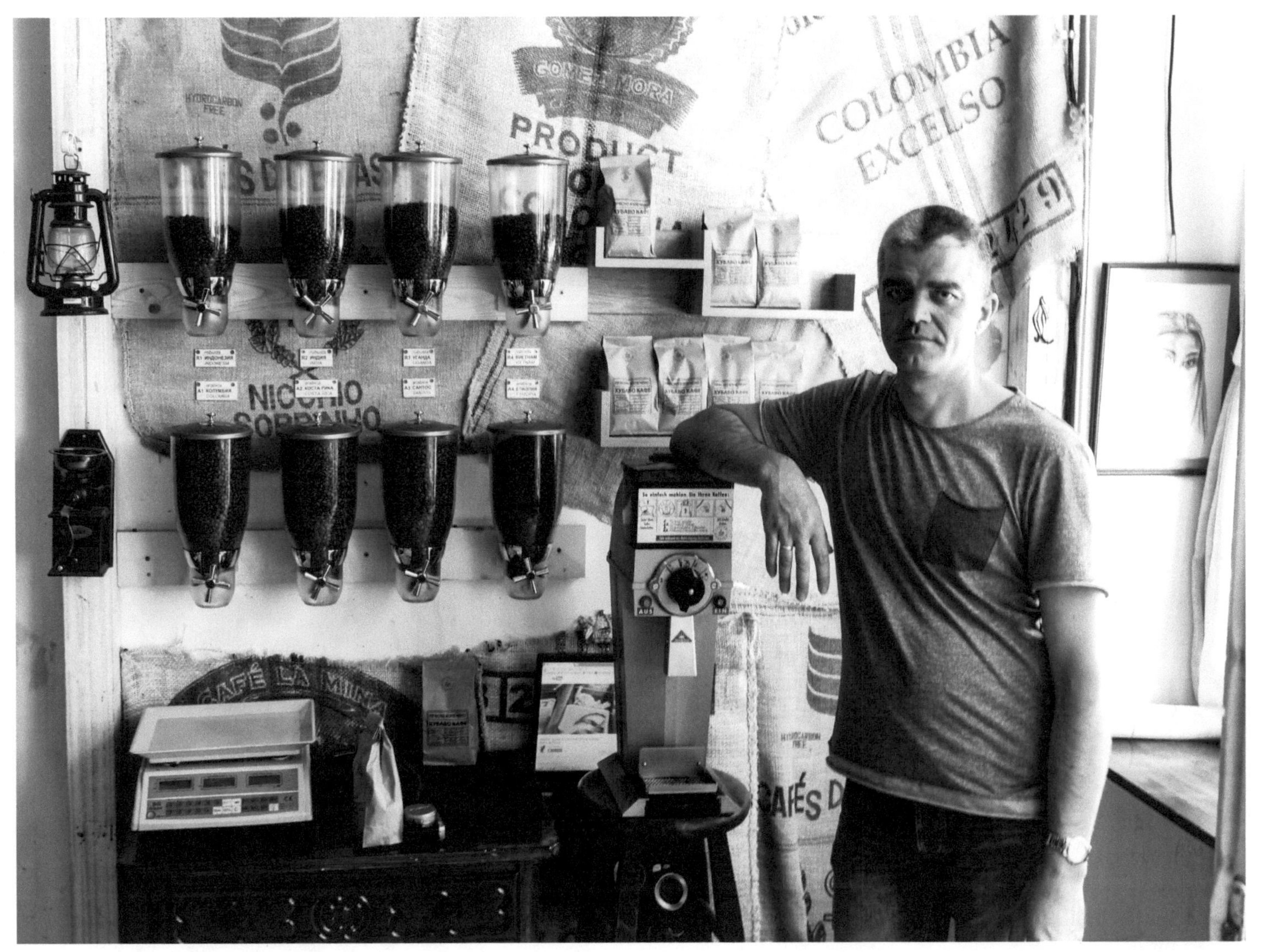

photograph by Paul Kelly

PLOVDIV, BULGARIA – Biblioteka Café. "This business is for the heart, not for money," says Angel Andreev at this hipster venue in Plovdiv which he co-owns.

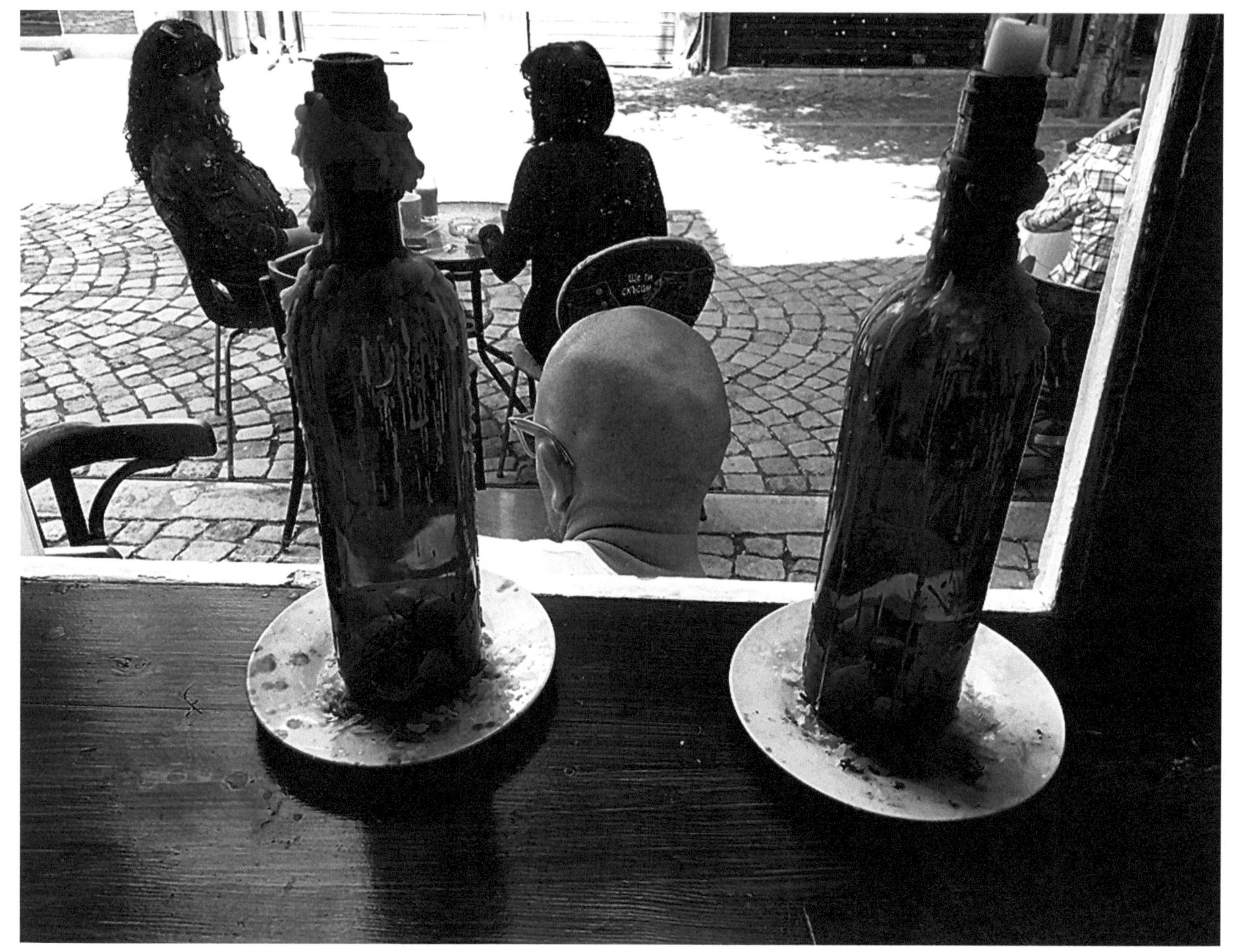

photograph by Fred Shively

PLOVDIV – Biblioteka Café. Slowly if not yet surely, café culture is coming back to Bulgaria.

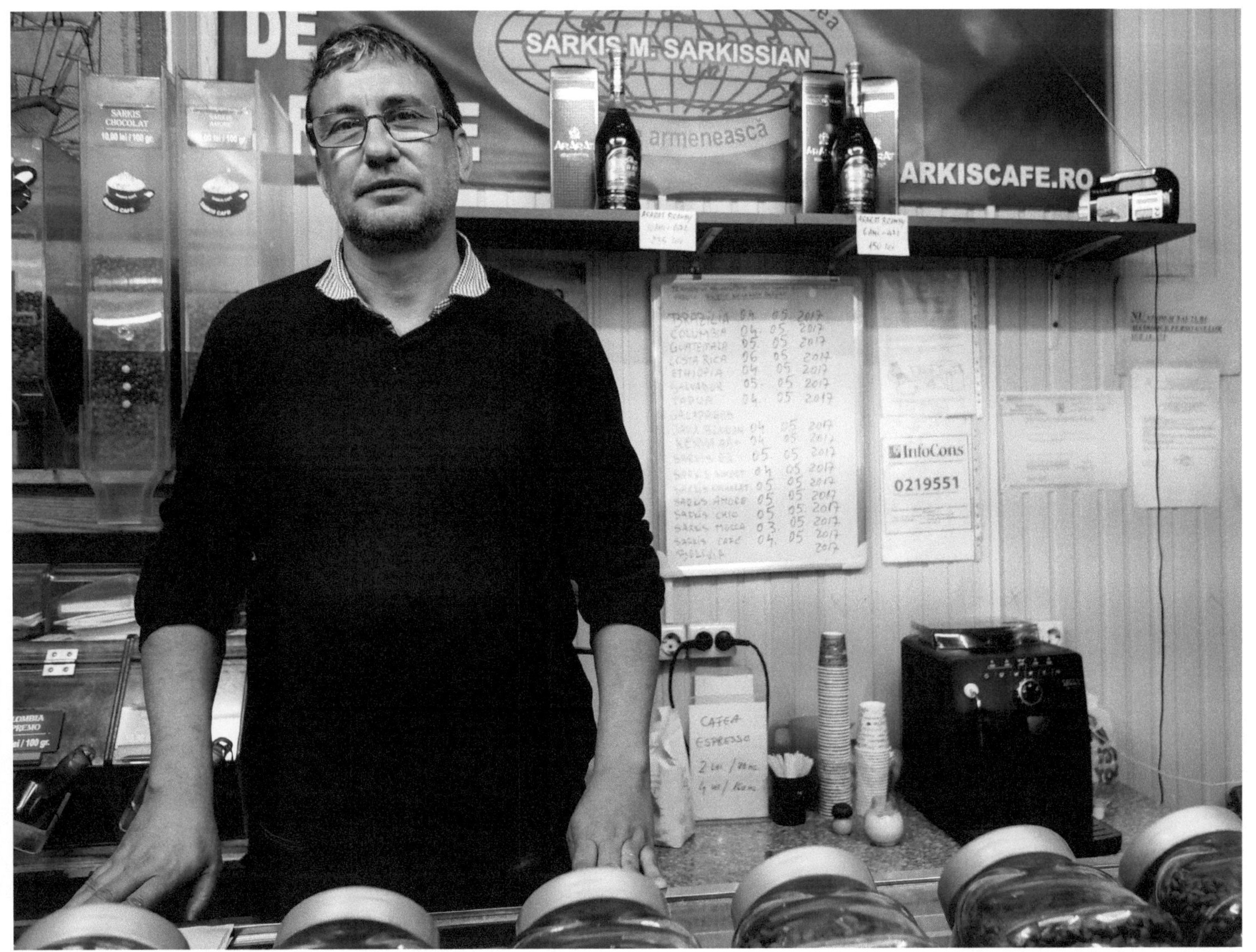

photograph by Paul Kelly

BUCHAREST, ROMANIA – the Armenian factor. If there is an old guard in Bucharest coffee culture, it can almost certainly be traced back to the Turkish Genocide against the Armenians in the early 1900s. Survivors of the Sarkissian and Macighian families, coffee shop proprietors from the old empire, took to the road and arrived in Romania where in 1912, at Ramnicu-Valcea, Bucharest, they set up two shops. Mihai Honciuc is the current proprietor of the original Sarkissian Café, still roasting, grinding and dispensing in traditional style.

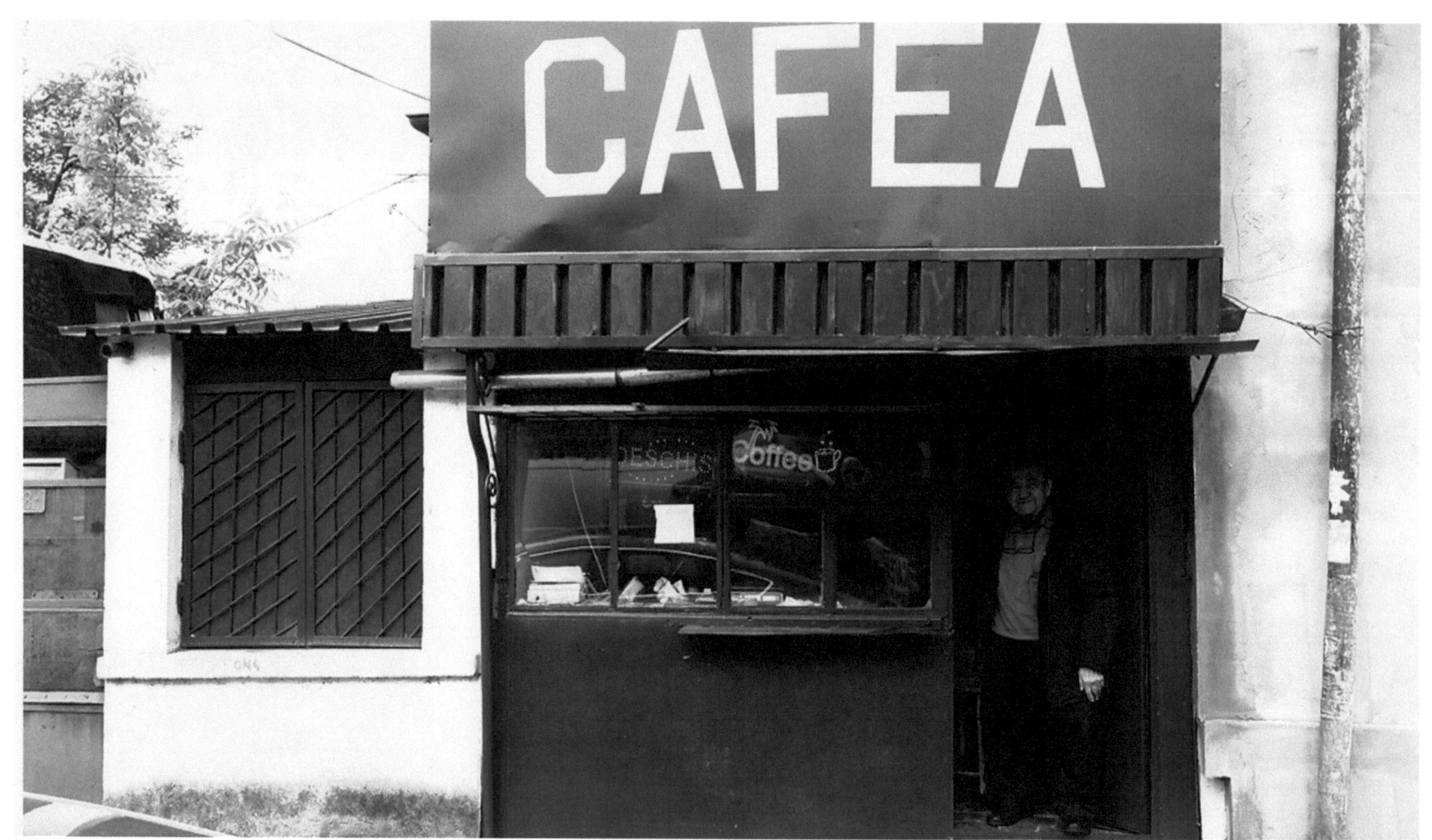

photograph by Fred Shively

BUCHAREST – the Armenian factor. Amidst equipment older than he is, 90 year old Haig Keskerian still serves a loyal customer base of diehard lovers of Armenian style blends from his tiny kiosk. Or did until he passed away on December 4th, 2017. Haig's much loved tiny kiosk will continue to provide Armenian style grinds and blends, thanks to a life-long friend.

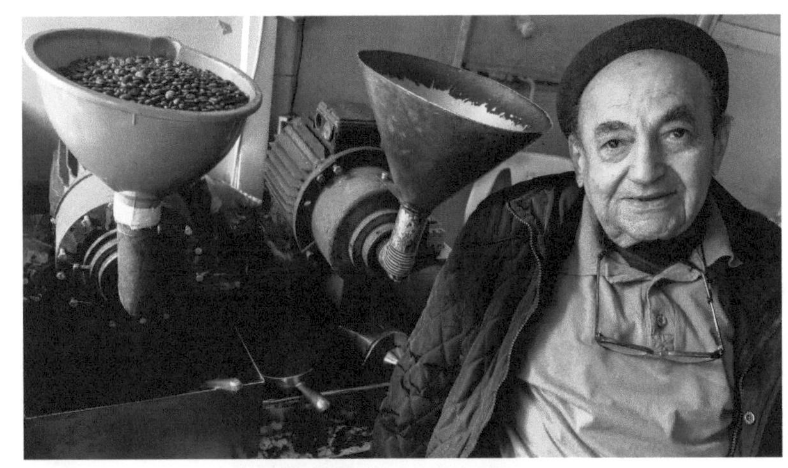

photograph by Paul Kelly

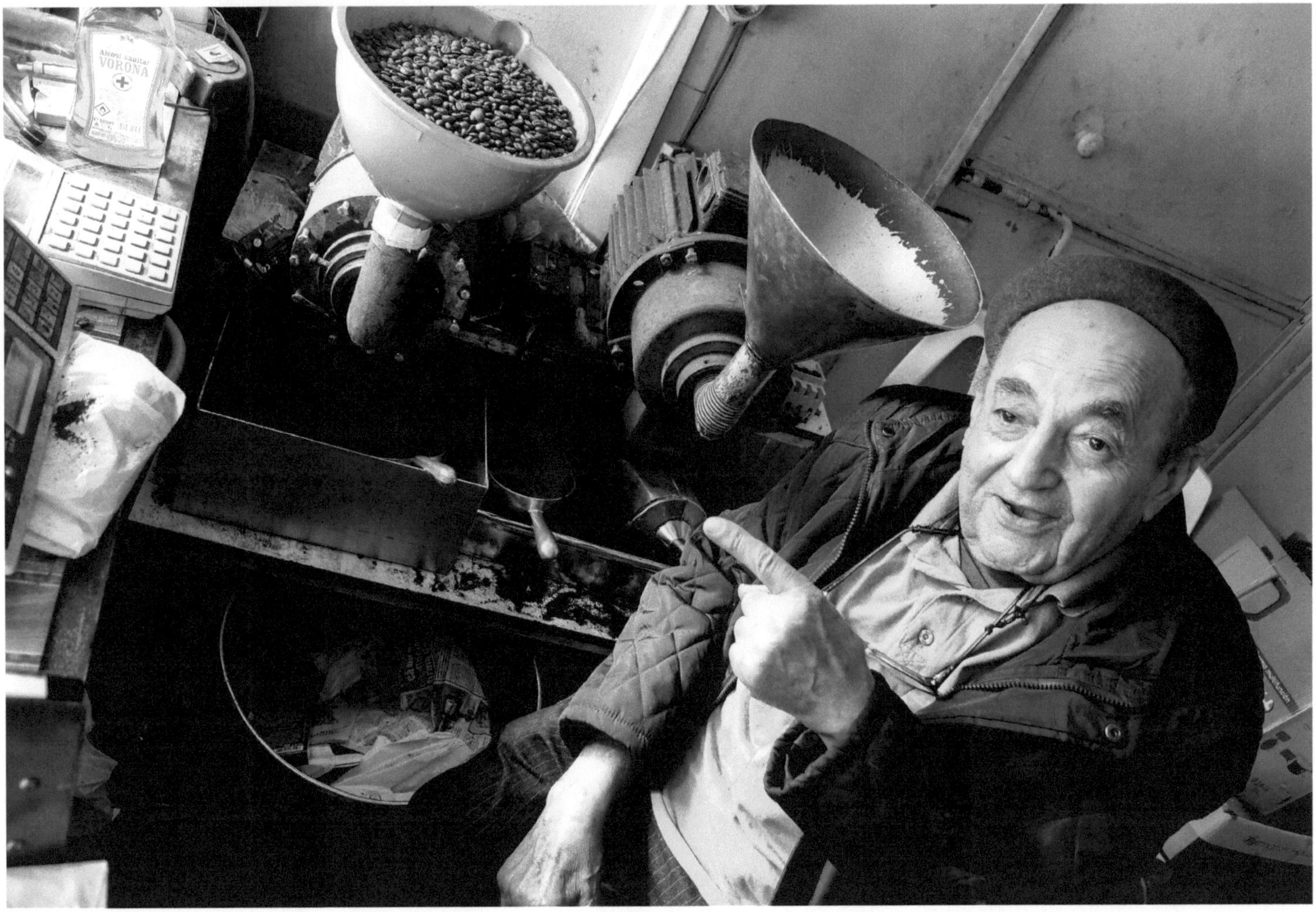

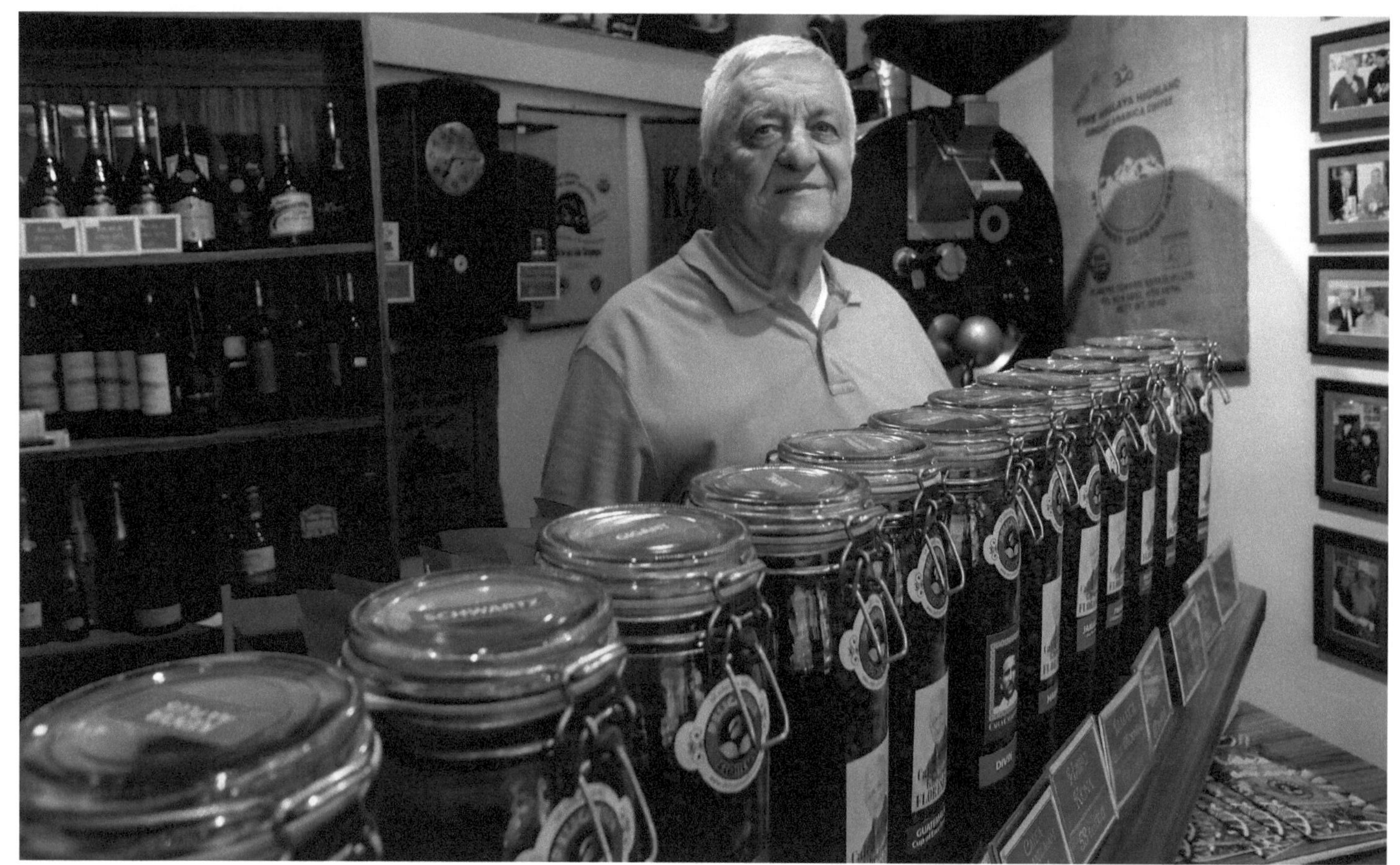

photograph by Paul Kelly

BUCHAREST – Delicatese Florescu. Perhaps the most renowned of the traditional Armenian coffee purveyors in Bucharest is Gheorge Florescu. His mentor Avedis Carabelaian, a former supplier of coffee to the Royal House of Romania, turned his family business over to his protégé Florescu some years before, and the business has continued to flourish.

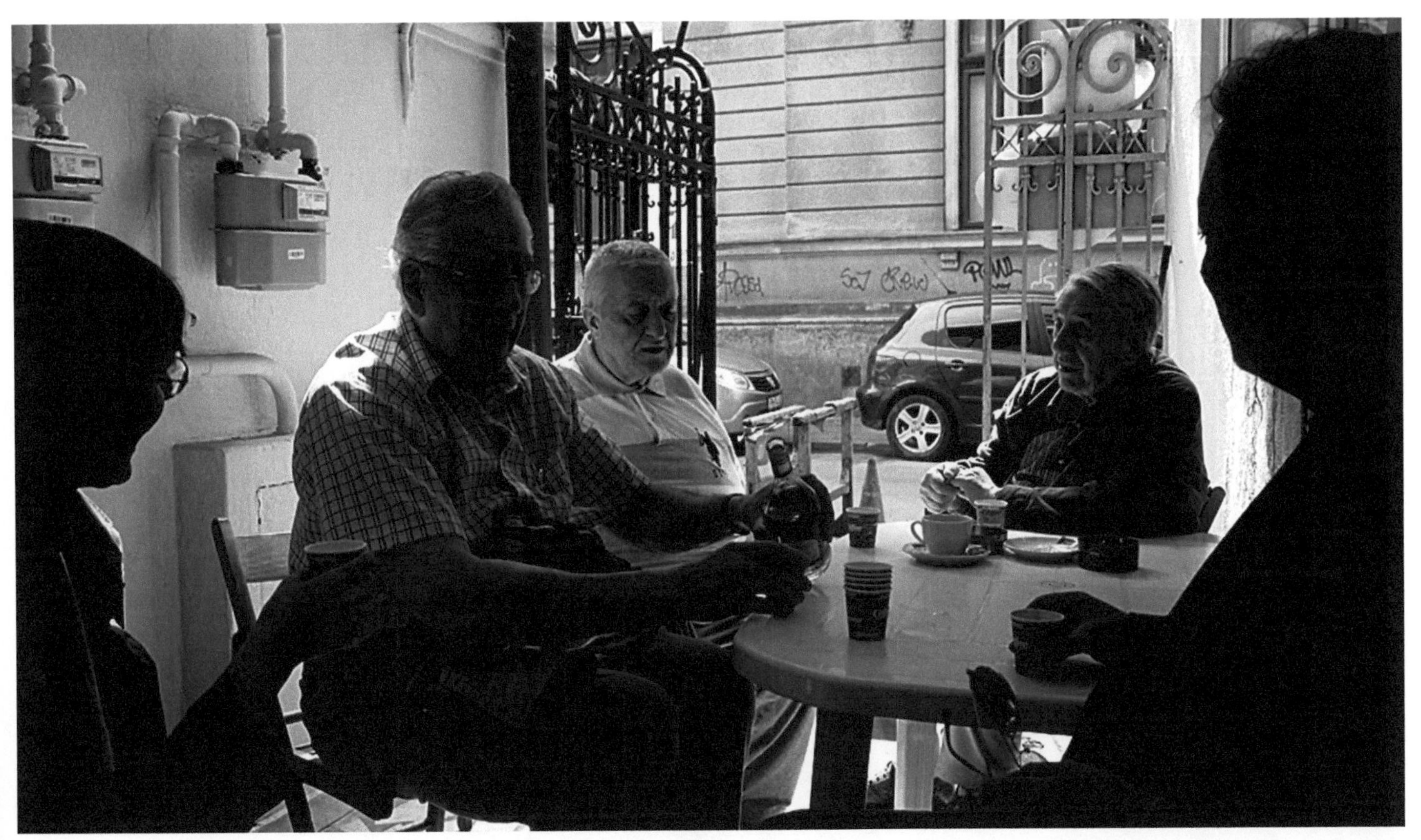

photograph by Fred Shively

BUCHAREST – Delicatese Florescu. Virtually every day, weather permitting, Gheorghe Florescu meets with friends for coffee in the passageway adjacent to the shop. On special occasions, a tot of famed Armenian Ararat brandy is served. This special occasion marks a visit from New York of Avedis Carabelian (pouring the brandy).

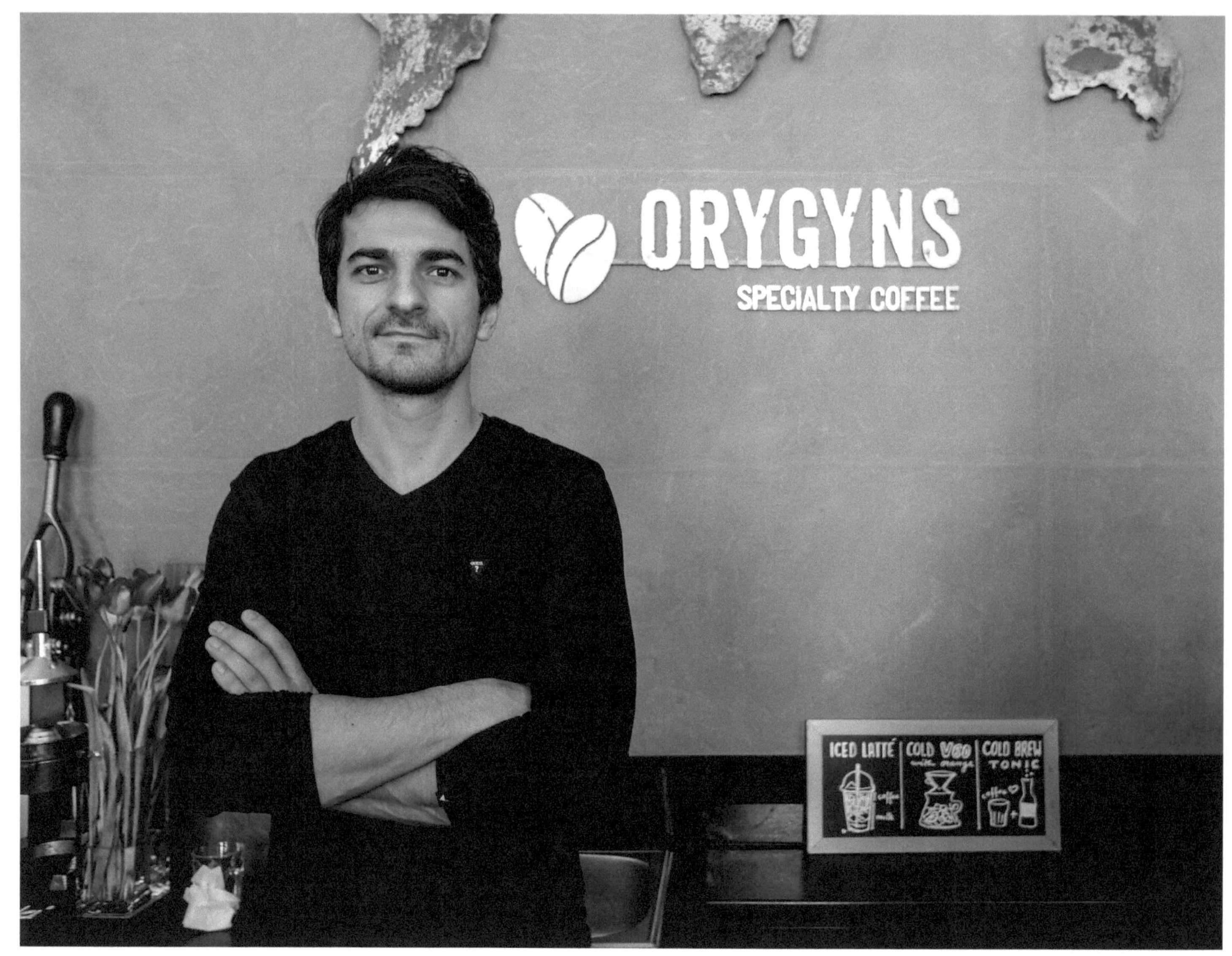

photograph by Paul Kelly

BUCHAREST – the third wave. Changing the traditions of coffee consumption in Romania has been challenging. Yet, in just a few years, specialty coffee has burst on to the scene all over the country, particularly in Bucharest. This is Cosmin Preda, suitably cool owner of a third-wave coffee house in the capital.

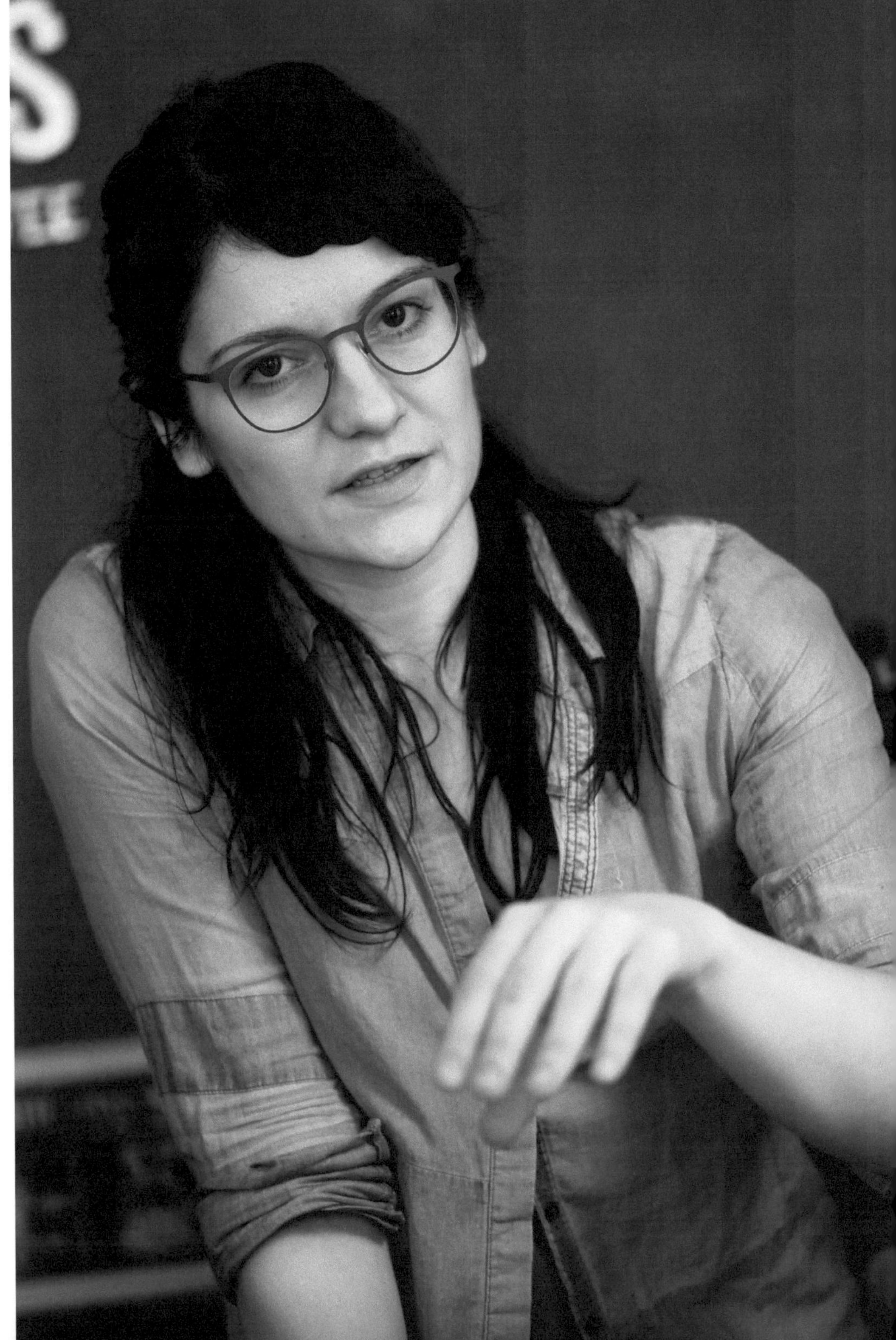

BUCHAREST – Orygyns. Orygyns' barista Sînziana Perțea describes how "people come in here to learn about coffee, to taste something new, they are really open to learning... Starbucks coffee is a dessert... it has its place, but we represent the third wave of cafés. We are about building a community and educating our customers".

photograph by Paul Kelly

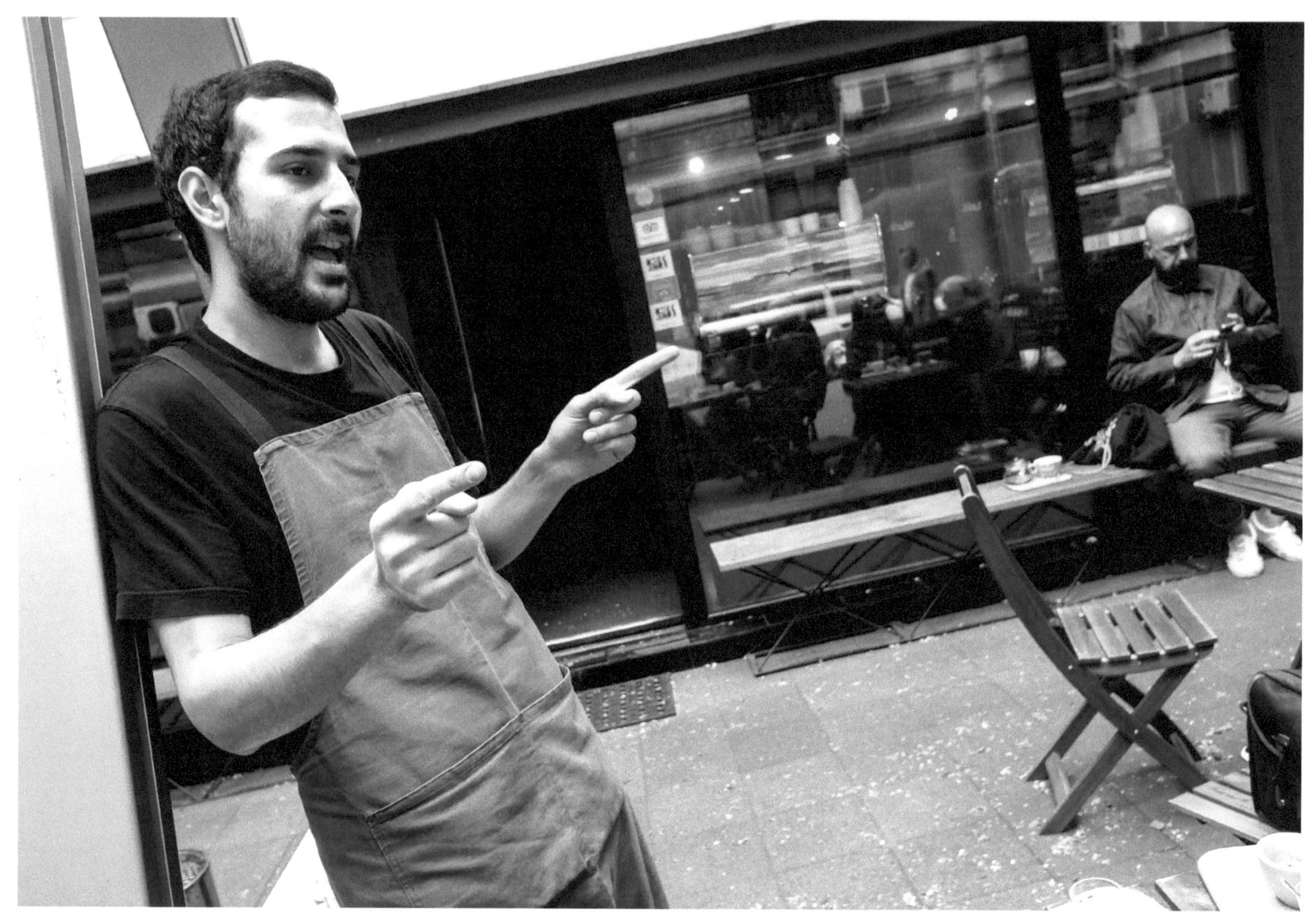

photograph by Paul Kelly

BUCHAREST - Origo. "We don't have waiters, everyone who works here is a certified barista. Third Wave cafes now require more interaction. Being a barista isn't just about making good coffee, you must be something of a showman as well". So says Victor, head Barista at Origo which claims to be Bucharest's first speciality café.

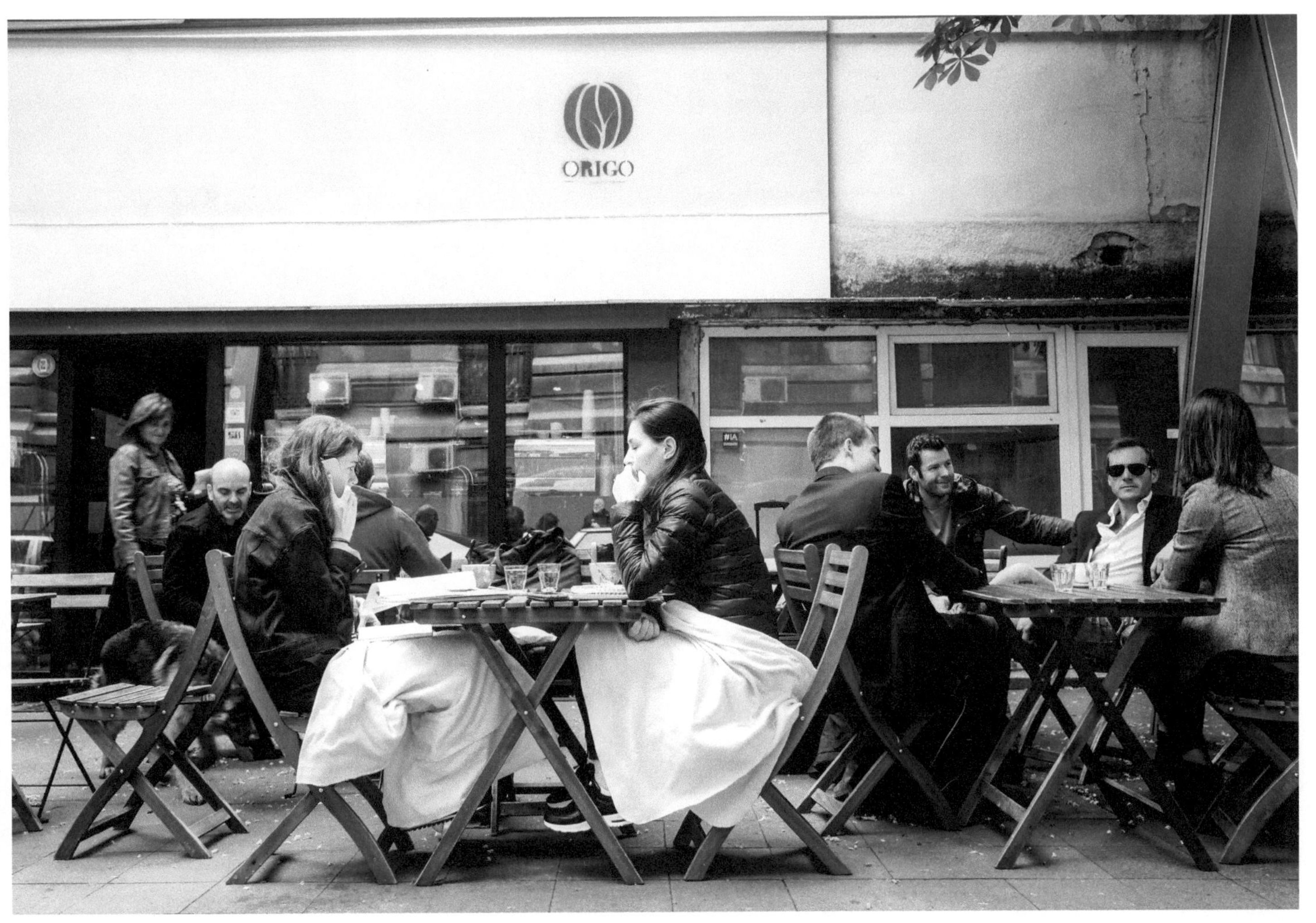

photograph by Paul Kelly

BUCHAREST – Origo. Sitting outside at a 'community table', head barista Victor reiterated what we heard all over Bulgaria: Communism all but destroyed the café culture. "But here in Romania we are changing all of that, it's coming back and it will be stronger than it ever was".

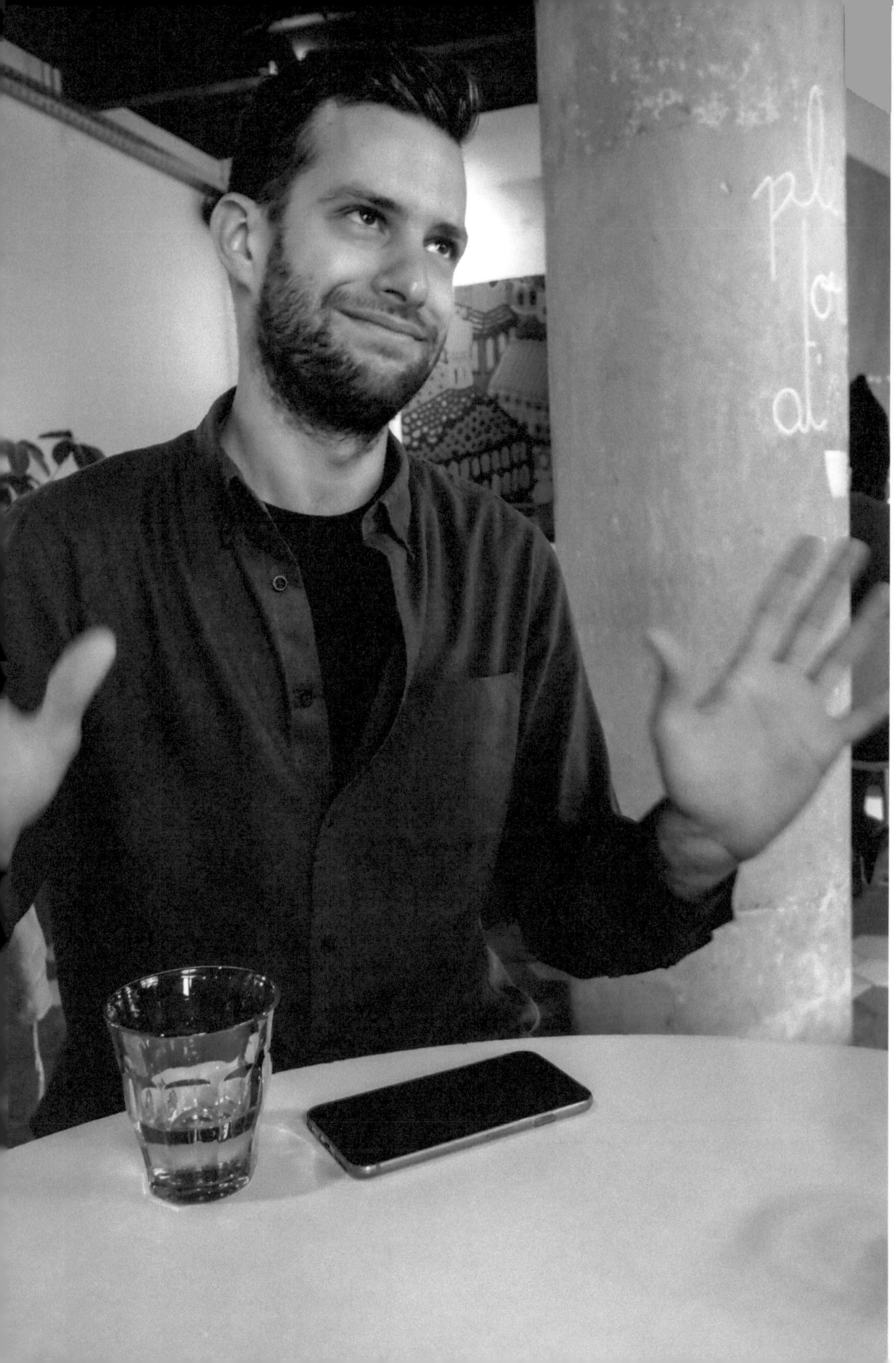

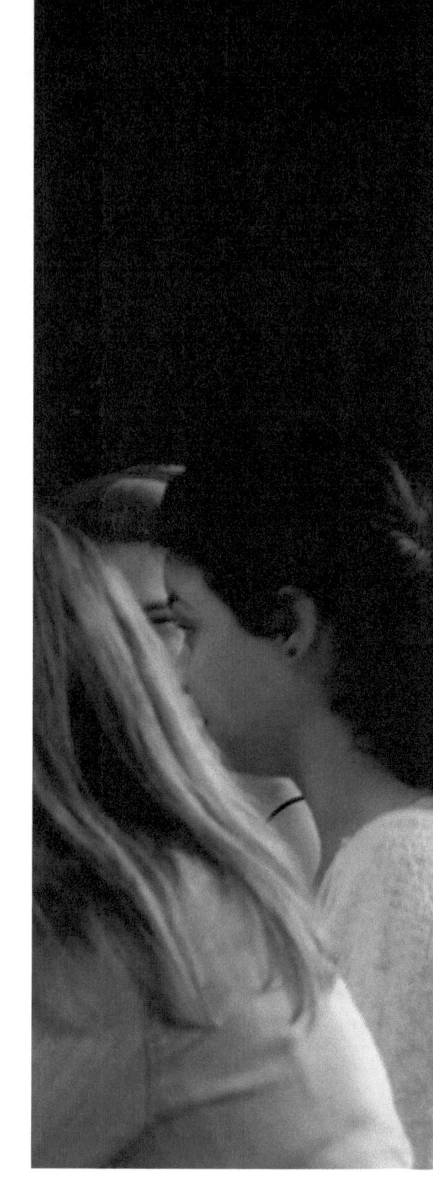

photograph by Paul Kelly

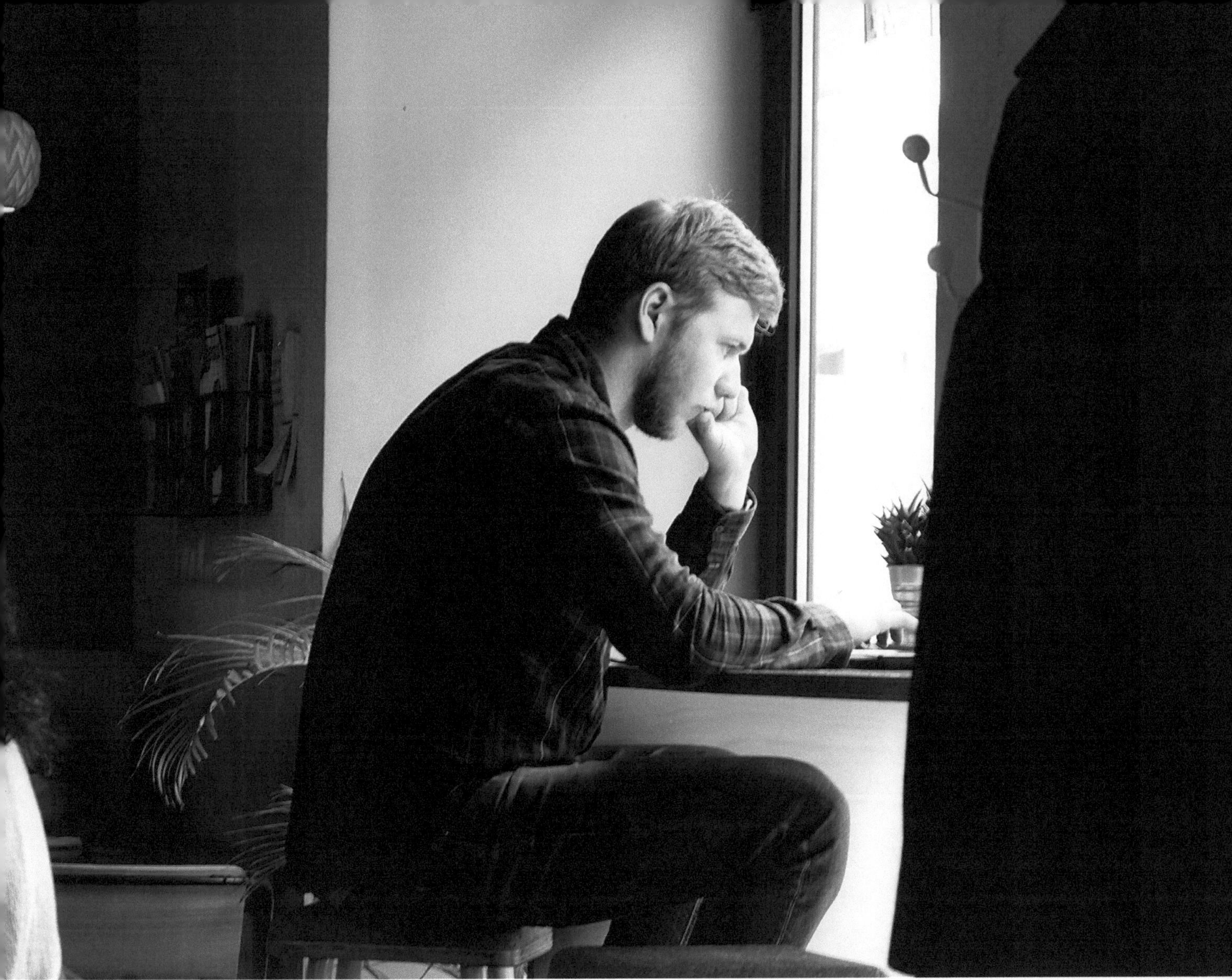

photograph by Fred Shively

BUCHAREST – M60 cafe. "Tradition for the sake of tradition isn't right,' says Razvan Crisan of the M60 Café, which he co-founded nearly three years ago. "Tradition is important as long as you don't gamble on value. M60 is hip and unpretentious and doesn't even bother using a logo, because we want customers to want to find us".

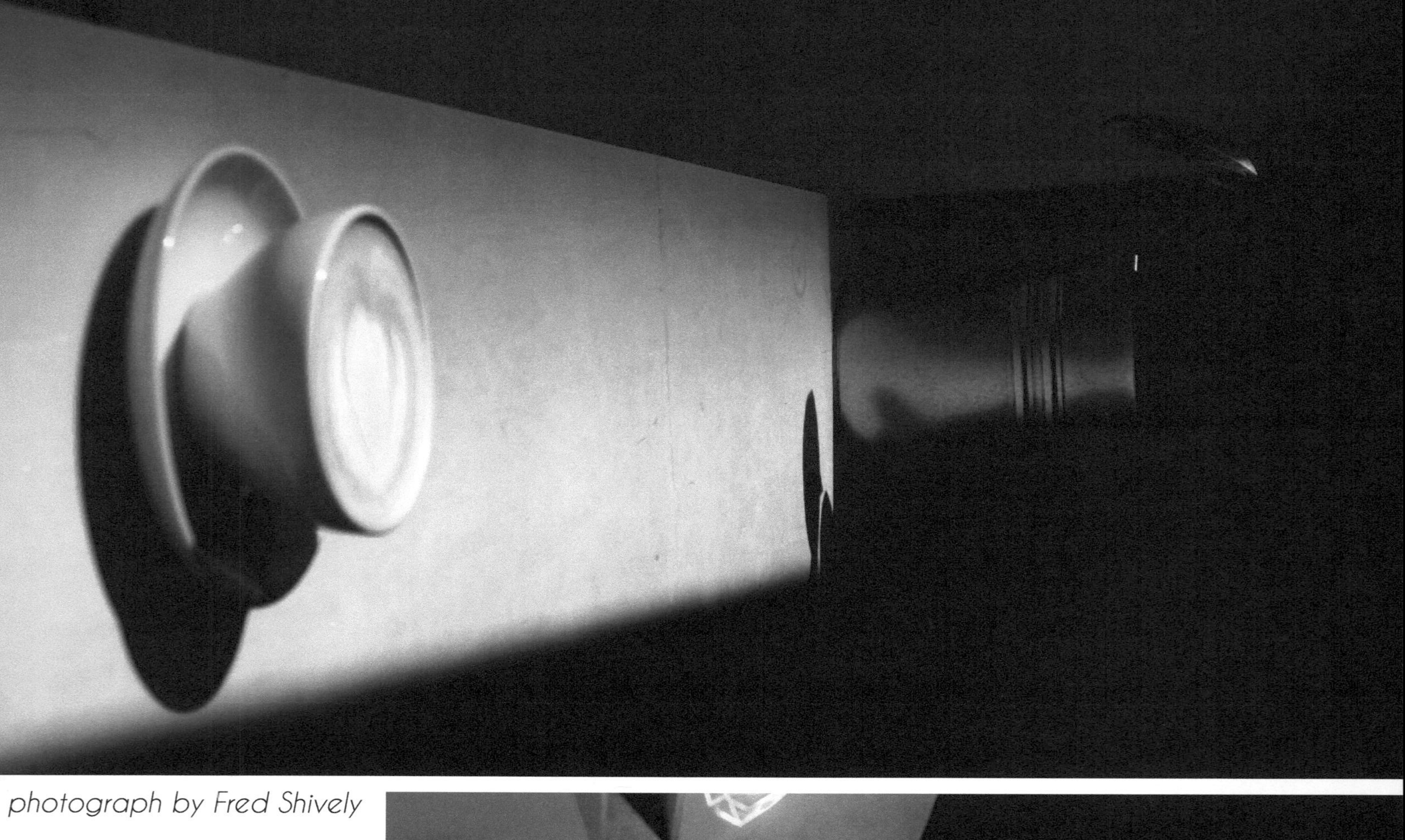

photograph by Fred Shively

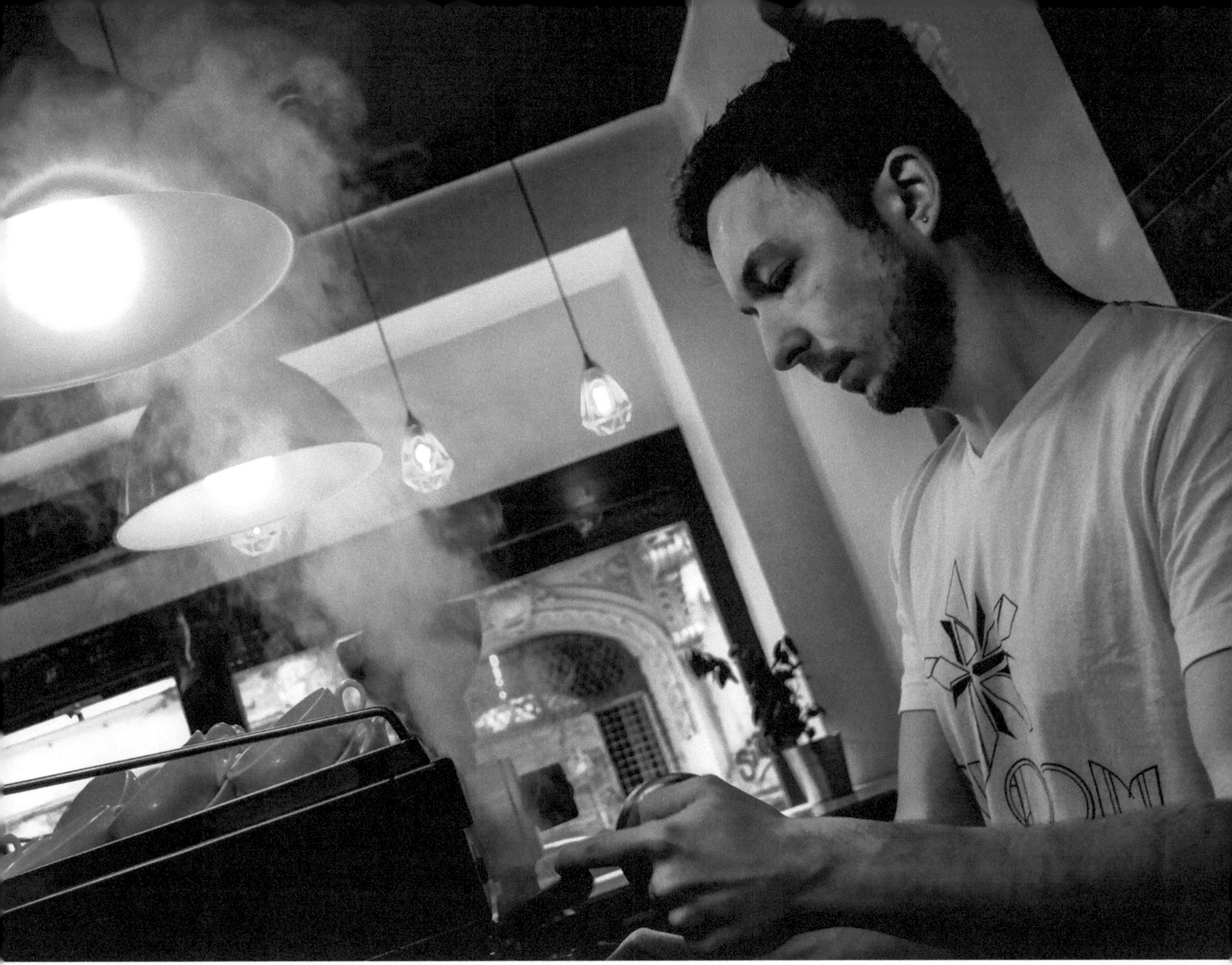

photograph by Paul Kelly

BUCHAREST – Bloom. When asked what makes Bloom stand out from the other speciality cafés that have sprung up in Bucharest over the last few years, barista Adrian says: "first it's about where and how the coffee is harvested; then the varietal and finally the process of roasting. And, of course, we grind all our own coffee".

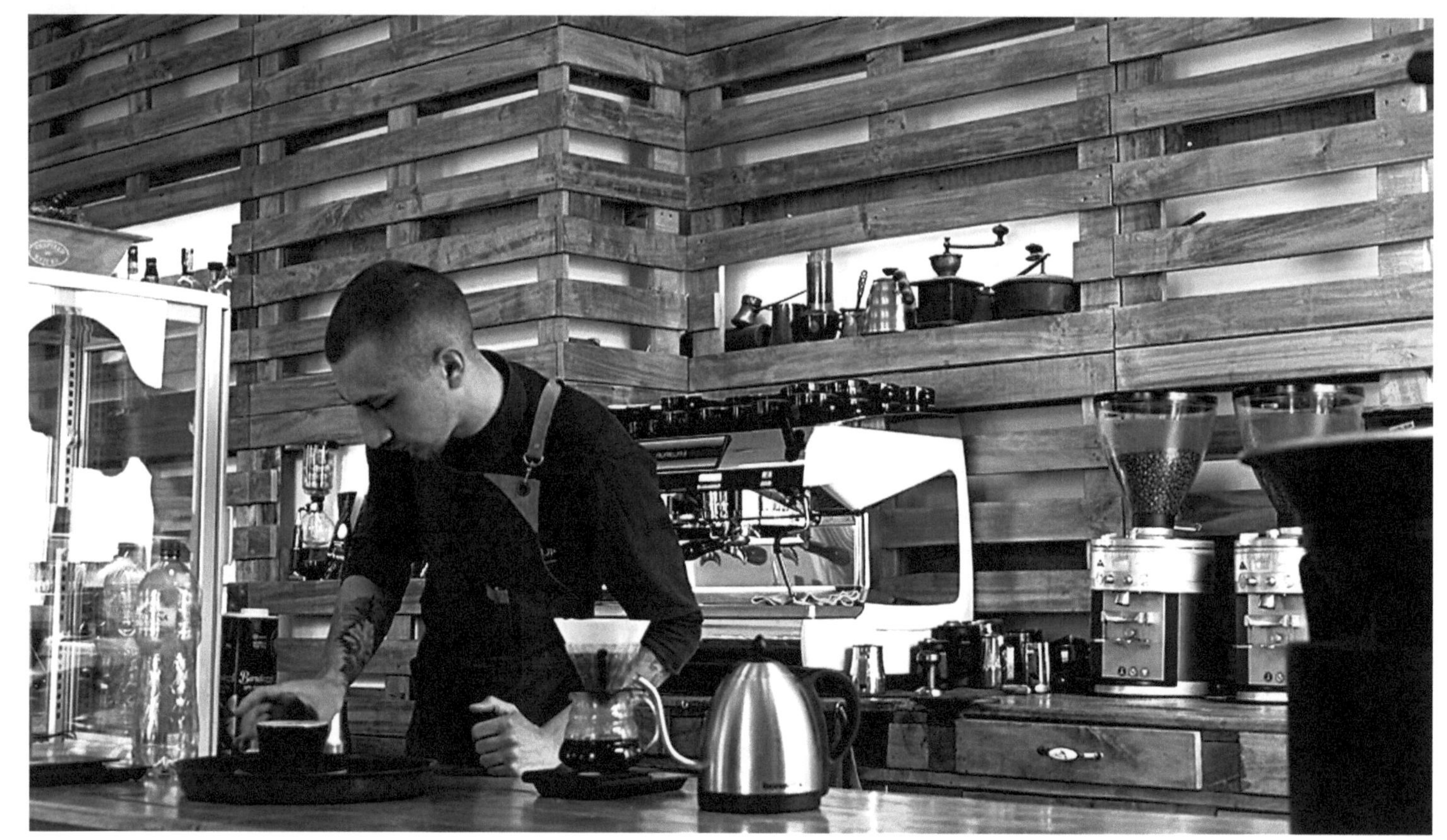

photograph by Fred Shively

CONSTANTA, ROMANIA - Haute Cup. "Romania's café culture was influenced by the Turks. Turkey, Macedonia and Greece all have strong café cultures. We'd like to be like them," says Alexander Wegner, owner of Haute Cup. If Bucharest's third wave café scene and Haute Cup in Constanta are anything to go by, Romania is well on its way to joining the cream of café society.

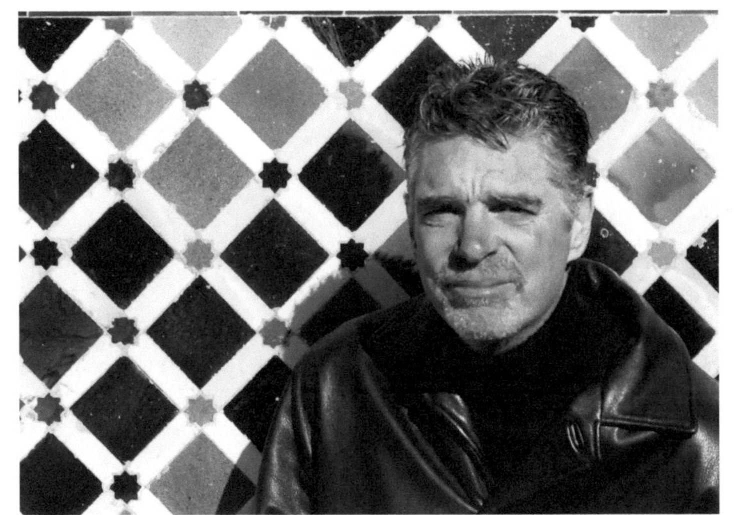

Paul Kelly

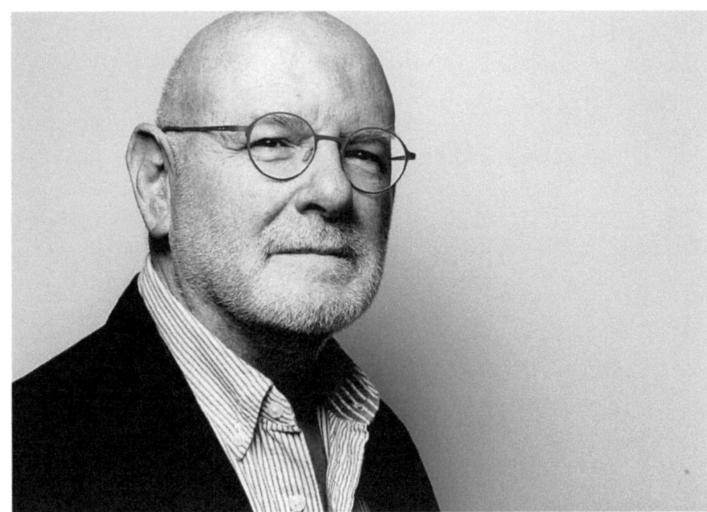

Fred Shively

Paul Kelly and Fred Shively have been professional communicators, sometimes photographers, always café/coffee lovers and insatiable travellers/flaneurs for more years than many of you have had... hot drinks.

Fred's background was in advertising and corporate communications and, latterly, travel photography and content. Some of Fred's work can be found at www.flickr.com/photos/fredshively

Paul's background was primarily in non-profit fundraising, although increasingly his photography is finding its way into a variety of global travel publications and sites. Have a look at some of his work at 500px.com/pmkphoto

Acknowledgments

When we were planning our Balkan Caffeination journey we were well aware of our lack of knowledge about the region, its people and culture, beyond what we were able to research and brief visits by Paul.

So the necessity of having excellent on-the-ground expertise quickly became apparent. We were very fortunate in our choice of people to fill that vacuum, with as knowledgeable and personable a group of guides as we could have wished for. People who 'got' what we were trying to achieve.

In Bosnia and Herzegovina, Ervin Tokic more than filled the bill with guidance, suggestions and anecdotes which brought Sarajevo and Mostar to life.

Kristina Stepanic shone a light on Serbia for us with delightful excursions to, in and around Loznica (her home town), Belgrade, Novi Sad and Valjevo.

Bulgaria, one of the tougher assignments, fell to Nadya Garbova, who even arranged a visit to her grandparents' home for a glimpse of Bulgarian home life and, in Sofia, took us underground for a curious encounter with the Bulgarian Photojournalists' Club of which she is a member.

In Romania, Cristina Josif ushered us to Bucharest's best New Wave cafés and helped us explore Constanta's caffeinated offerings in Romania's premier Black Sea resort.

Providing wisdom, chuckles and companionship, was our friend Saad Souissi who had played a similar role on a previous excursion through Eastern Europe some years earlier.

We chose not to hire a vehicle. On this trip we did not want to navigate thousands of kilometres, or figure out forest trails and snaking mountain roads. Especially, we did not want to encounter the hazards of city traffic in Belgrade, Sofia and Bucharest. Instead, we chose to hire drivers. These were organised by the aforementioned guides and proved to be invaluable as well as great – and informative – company.

Finally, a big thank you to Arpi Armenakian Shively, who copy-edited and proofread the sparse, but important descriptive copy that accompanies our images.

Fred & Paul

www.ingramcontent.com/pod-product-compliance
Lightning Source LLC
LaVergne TN
LVHW071630100826
845154LV00007BA/122
* 9 7 8 1 9 1 2 7 7 7 0 4 4 *